ISRAEL

ISRAEL
A BIBLICAL VIEW

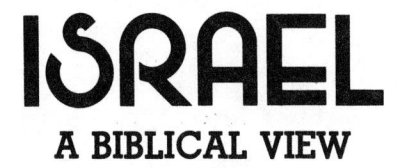

By
William Sanford LaSor

William B. Eerdmans Publishing Company
Grand Rapids, Michigan

Copyright © 1976 by William Sanford LaSor
All rights reserved
Printed in the United States of America

Library of Congress Cataloging in Publication Data

La Sor, William Sanford.
  Israel.

  1. Servant of Jehovah—Addresses, essays, lectures.
2. Bible—History of Biblical events—Addresses,
essays, lectures. 3. Bible. O.T. Prophets—
Criticism, interpretation, etc.—Addresses, essays,
lectures. 4. Church—Biblical teaching—Addresses,
essays, lectures. I. Title.
BS1199.S4L3   221.8'95694   75-46520
ISBN 0-8028-1635-X

The Scripture quotations in this publication are from the Revised Standard Version of the Bible, copyrighted 1946, 1952, © 1971, 1973 by the Division of Christian Education of the National Council of the Churches of Christ in the U.S.A., and used by permission.

To
BETSY "JUNIOR"
this work
is affectionately dedicated

רַבּוֹת בָּנוֹת עָשׂוּ חָיִל
וְאַתְּ עָלִית עַל־כֻּלָּנָה:

Proverbs 31:29

PREFACE

What thoughts does the word "Israel" conjure up in our minds? In view of the frequent items in the press and other news media, we think first of all, perhaps, of the modern State of Israel. I have many friends in Israel. For a short while I lived among them, and on other occasions I have visited them. My life is richer because of such experiences.

I have many dear friends also who live in the neighboring Arab countries. Some of them—perhaps most of them—will be somewhat offended by the title. There is far too much emotional charge in the word "Israel." I have attended worship in churches in Arab countries, as well as carol services at the Shepherds' Field in Bethlehem and Easter services at the Garden Tomb in Jerusalem. I noticed that the words "Israel" and "Zion" were carefully avoided, and some familiar hymns were paraphrased to eliminate these terms. One friend told me that it is almost impossible to use the Old Testament in an Arab Christian service. Of course, this is understandable, for I have lived among my Arab friends, too, and visited them many times. I am quite aware of their sensitivity on this subject. But for God's people, this should not be. The term "Israel," like the Old Testament, belongs to all of us.

Therefore I would like to discuss the subject "Israel." The subject has interested me for many years, in fact long before there was a State of Israel. The word "Israel" occurs over 2500 times in the Old Testament, and about 68 times in the New Testament—facts which amply indicate the importance of the subject. The term is used of individuals, of a family or clan, of a nation, of a split-off nation which we sometimes call "the northern kingdom," and of a spiritual concept. In our study we shall attempt to learn something about this multifaceted word.

Various portions of this work have been given in many different places and in several different forms: classroom lectures of course, studies in adult Bible classes, sermons, portions of books and articles, and so on. When my good friend and former student, Rev. Albert C. Strong, pastor of the First Presbyterian Church of Sanger, California, invited me to give a series on "Israel," I had the opportunity to organize the material and cast it in the present form. Later, when Dr. Lloyd H. Newlin invited me to present the same studies in the First Baptist Church of Torrance, California, I was able to work through the material once again, and make some refinements. The studies were recorded and transcribed, and then were edited. I have deliberately tried to retain as much as possible of the characteristics of the spoken word.

Here I would like to record my thanks to all who had a share in making a book out of the spoken words. The warm reception which the messages have had, and the expressions that suggested publication of them, were an encouragement of course, and I am grateful. Transcribing recorded messages which contain unusual terms, lots of Scripture quotations (usually with no indication where they would be found, and often from a memory that confuses the words of various translations as well as my own idea of what the Hebrew intends to say), with no indication of punctuation and sentence or paragraph division, is a task that many secretaries seek to avoid. I therefore wish to express very warm appreciation to Dolores M. Loeding for this faithful service. If there were others in our secretarial pool that shared this responsibility unbeknownst to me, I certainly thank them, too. Yvonne A. Geiger typed the final draft for the printer and made my task of proofreading unusually easy. A special word of appreciation to Marguerite L. Shuster is in order. The request for publication of this little volume came at a time when I was under a very heavy burden of work on other commitments, and Miss Shuster has done a splendid job of editing my hastily revised draft from the material transcribed from the tapes. Usually, I revise and rewrite a manuscript several times—which in this case was simply impossible. I therefore am greatly indebted to Marguerite for taking much of the burden from me.

Scripture quotations, unless otherwise indicated, are taken from the Revised Standard Version.

With the prayer that the Lord may see fit to use this work to develop a greater interest in Israel, and a deeper understanding of the very rich religious content of the word, I send it forth.

William Sanford LaSor

Fuller Theological Seminary

CONTENTS

Preface	6
1. The Servant of the Lord	11
2. Israel in History	30
3. Israel in Prophecy	55
4. The Church as Israel	83

CHAPTER ONE

THE SERVANT OF THE LORD

Who is the Servant of the Lord? This question has occupied the minds of Bible students for centuries. It was the question which the Ethiopian government official put to Philip (Acts 8). The Ethiopian, we remember, was returning from Jerusalem. Since he had been there "to worship," we can conclude that he was one of the numerous Gentiles at the turn of the era who had become a worshiper of the God of the Jews. The Spirit of God prompted Philip to join the Ethiopian in his chariot, and as he approached, Philip heard him reading the portion of Isaiah that says,

> "As a sheep led to the slaughter
> or a lamb before its shearer is dumb,
> so he opens not his mouth.
> In his humiliation justice was denied him.
> Who can describe his generation?
> For his life is taken up from the earth."
> (Acts 8:32–33)

Philip asked, "Do you understand what you are reading?" (Acts 8:30). The Ethiopian replied, "How can I, unless some one guides me?" (8:31). The Ethiopian asked then specifically, "About whom does the prophet say this, about himself or about some one else?" (8:34).

Jewish scholars have asked the same question. So have Christian scholars. In an exquisitely beautiful, poetic passage Isaiah has given the world these words:

> Behold, my servant shall prosper,
>> he shall be exalted and lifted up,
>> and shall be very high.
> As many were astonished at him—
>> his appearance was so marred, beyond human semblance,
>> and his form beyond that of the sons of men—
> so shall he startle many nations;
>> kings shall shut their mouths because of him;
> for that which has not been told them they shall see,
>> and that which they have not heard they shall understand.
>
> Who has believed what we have heard?
>> And to whom has the arm of the Lord been revealed?
> For he grew up before him like a young plant,
>> and like a root out of dry ground;
> he had no form or comeliness that we should look at him,
>> and no beauty that we should desire him.
> He was despised and rejected by men;
>> a man of sorrows, and acquainted with grief;
> and as one from whom men hide their faces
>> he was despised, and we esteemed him not.
>
> Surely he has borne our griefs
>> and carried our sorrows;

yet we esteemed him stricken,
> smitten by God, and afflicted.

But he was wounded for our transgressions,
> he was bruised for our iniquities;

upon him was the chastisement that made us whole,
> and with his stripes we are healed.

All we like sheep have gone astray;
> we have turned every one to his own way;

and the Lord has laid on him
> the iniquity of us all.

He was oppressed, and he was afflicted,
> yet he opened not his mouth;

like a lamb that is led to the slaughter,
> and like a sheep that before its shearers is dumb,
> so he opened not his mouth.

By oppression and judgment he was taken away;
> and as for his generation, who considered

that he was cut off out of the land of the living,
> stricken for the transgression of my people?

And they made his grave with the wicked
> and with a rich man in his death,

although he had done no violence,
> and there was no deceit in his mouth.

Yet it was the will of the Lord to bruise him;
> he has put him to grief;

when he makes himself an offering for sin,
> he shall see his offspring, he shall prolong his days;

the will of the Lord shall prosper in his hand;
> he shall see the fruit of the travail of his soul and be satisfied;

by his knowledge shall the righteous one, my servant,

>   make many to be accounted righteous;
>   and he shall bear their iniquities.
>   Therefore I will divide him a portion with the great,
>   and he shall divide the spoil with the strong;
>   because he poured out his soul to death,
>   and was numbered with the transgressors;
>   yet he bore the sin of many,
>   and made intercession for the transgressors.
> >   (Isaiah 52:13—53:12)

The prophet was speaking to people who were living in hard times. They had been defeated by the enemy. Some of them had gone into captivity. The prophet had been inspired to proclaim this encouraging message:

>   Comfort, comfort my people,
>   says your God.
>   Speak tenderly to Jerusalem,
>   and cry to her
>   that her warfare is ended,
>   that her iniquity is pardoned,
>   that she has received from the Lord's hand
>   double for all her sins.
>
>   * * *
>
>   Behold, the Lord God comes with might,
>   and his arm rules for him;
>   behold, his reward is with him,
>   and his recompense before him.
>   He will feed his flock like a shepherd,
>   he will gather the lambs in his arms,
>   he will carry them in his bosom,
>   and gently lead those that are with young.
> >   (Isaiah 40:1—2, 10—11)

In the chapters of Isaiah that follow, the prophet sets forth the great truth, one of the greatest in the

ISRAEL

Old Testament, that the God of Israel, the Lord, Yahweh, is the only God, creator and ruler of the whole world. This tremendous truth is proclaimed in ways that are clearer and more emphatic than previous statements had been. To a people who had suffered terrible defeat, the prophet declared that their God was greater than all other gods. In fact, the gods of the nations, including those of Babylonia, were nothing. They were idols made of gold and silver and wood and stone. They were the work of men's hands. But the God of Israel was the Maker of all things. He was even the Maker of those who made the idols. A magnificent doctrine! The prophet says,

> Have you not known? Have you not heard?
> The Lord is the everlasting God,
> > the Creator of the ends of the earth.
> He does not faint or grow weary,
> > his understanding is unsearchable.
> > > (Isaiah 40:28)

> It is he...
> who brings princes to nought,
> > and makes the rulers of the earth as nothing.
> > > (Isaiah 40:22-23)

The prophet then goes on to speak of the Servant of the Lord, a subject which he pursues through chapters 41 to 53 of Isaiah. There are three, or four, or five passages—the number varies according to the opinions of scholars—which may be described as poems that discuss, or talk about, or include conversation with, the Servant of the Lord. According to one analysis, the "Servant Songs" can be found in these passages:

> Isaiah 42:1–4 (perhaps to v. 7)
> Isaiah 49:1–6
> Isaiah 50:4–9
> Isaiah 52:13–53:12

However, a careful reading of the entire section, extending from chapter 41 (not 42) through chapter 53, will show that it is *all* about the Servant of the Lord. But who is this servant?

1

According to some careful Bible students, the Servant of the Lord is Israel. This identification certainly is correct. Isaiah himself gives this interpretation:

> But you, Israel, my servant,
>> Jacob, whom I have chosen,
>> the offspring of Abraham, my friend;
> you whom I took from the ends of the earth,
>> and called from its farthest corners,
> saying to you, "You are my servant,
>> I have chosen you and not cast you off";
> fear not, for I am with you,
>> be not dismayed, for I am your God;
> I will strengthen you, I will help you,
>> I will uphold you with my victorious right hand.
>
> (Isaiah 41:8–10)

Israel, the people who descended from Abraham through Isaac and Jacob, who had been delivered from Egyptian bondage, who had been established in the land of the Canaanites, and who then had been ravaged by the Assyrians and utterly destroyed by the Babylonians—Israel was the people chosen by the Lord. Israel was his servant.

ISRAEL

His purpose in selecting Israel is suggested in the following chapter in these words:

> Behold my servant, whom I uphold,
>   my chosen, in whom my soul delights;
> I have put my Spirit upon him,
>   he will bring forth justice to the nations.
>   (Isaiah 42:1)

The word translated "chosen" is the same word as the one translated "elect." When we speak of Israel as God's "chosen people," we are using the same term as that used when we speak of election—God's election of the people of Israel.

Election is a theological issue that has been badly handled and is therefore very much mistrusted by some students of the Bible. According to a popular misunderstanding, the election of Israel is an end in itself. God chose Israel out of all the nations of the world in order to bless this people, and—by inference—in order to send the rest of the world to hell. That sort of procedure is not what the Bible doctrine of election is all about. The passage in Isaiah (42:1) is perfectly clear provided we don't try to "make it clearer." The Lord says that his servant, the one "in whom my soul delights," is the recipient of God's special blessing for a purpose: "he will bring forth justice to the nations."

From the Old Testament point of view, the world was divided into two groups, Israel and the "nations." The word that is translated "nation" is often translated "Gentile." Anyone who is not an Israelite is a Gentile. (We might add that sometimes even Israel is called a "nation," and Abraham was told that he would become the father of a multitude of "Gentiles," Gen. 17:4.) God chose the Israelites so that they might make known to the rest of the nations his truth, his justice.

> "I am the Lord, I have called you in righteousness,
>   I have taken you by the hand and kept you;
> I have given you as a covenant to the people,
>   a light to the nations...."
>
> (Isaiah 42:6)

To be "a light to the nations," to the Gentiles—this was the purpose of Israel's election.

Of course, this purpose was no new revelation given to the prophet. It was the purpose originally announced when the Lord called Abram in Ur of the Chaldees. God said to Abram, "Go from your country and your kindred and your father's house to the land that I will show you. And I will make of you a great nation [a great Gentile!], and I will bless you, and make your name great; so be a blessing!" (Gen. 12:1–2; the last clause I have translated literally, for the Hebrew is clearly an imperative). God continues to say, "and in you all the families of the earth will be blessed" (Gen. 12:3, RSV mg). Israel's election was not an end, but rather a means to an end. Israel was chosen in order that the world—the gentile world that knew not the true God—might have light, might be made to see, might have understanding of the great redemptive love of God.

But Israel had been a blind and disobedient servant. This is the prophet's description:

> Hear, you deaf;
>   and look, you blind, that you may see!
> Who is blind but my servant,
>   or deaf as my messenger whom I send?

ISRAEL

> Who is blind as my dedicated one,
> or blind as the servant of the Lord?
> He sees many things, but does not observe them;
> his ears are open, but he does not hear.
>
> (Isaiah 42:18–20)

It was the Lord's intention to "magnify his law and make it glorious" (42:21). He is the Maker of the earth and all things in it; who should know better what is best for all creatures? The maker of a fine machine states the operating conditions that will give optimum performance. These conditions are the "law" of the manufacturer. God's law sets forth the conditions that will best serve the common weal, and his servant was supposed to show forth that law. Instead, Israel refused to walk in the ways of the Lord. Israel refused to obey his laws. The Lord looked for justice, and he saw bloodshed. He looked for righteousness, but "behold, a cry!" (Isa. 5:7). Finally, after having sent his prophets for several generations to proclaim his word to Israel, God was forced to punish his unfaithful servant.

> So he poured upon him the heat of his anger
> and the might of battle. . . .
>
> (Isaiah 42:25)

Even that failed to turn his servant to the Lord's way. The disobedient servant Israel can hardly be the one of whom the prophet speaks in chapter 53.

2

At the end of chapter 44, God says of Cyrus the king of Persia, "He is my shepherd, and he shall fulfil all my purpose" (44:28). In the following verse, the prophet refers to Cyrus as the Lord's "anointed": the Hebrew word that is used is the word from which we get "Messiah" (45:1). Some students of the Servant Songs have therefore concluded that Cyrus was the Servant of the Lord.

Let us reword that statement slightly: Cyrus was *a* servant of the Lord. He was the Lord's shepherd. In the plan of the God who rules all nations, Cyrus was to fulfil the Lord's purpose. Included in that purpose is the rebuilding of Jerusalem and the laying of the foundation of the temple (44:28). The Lord referring to Cyrus says, "whose right hand I have grasped" (45:1). Grasping of the hands by the king and the idol, the symbol of deity, was an established custom in Mesopotamia, implying that the king served the god and the god protected the king. The Lord promised to "subdue nations" and "ungird the loins of kings" before Cyrus. The Lord would "go before" Cyrus, and "level the mountains." He would deliver into the hands of Cyrus "the treasures of darkness and the hoards in secret places." The Lord said to Cyrus, "I call you by your name ... though you do not know me" (45:1–4).

These are amazing statements! Where else in the Old Testament—or in the entire Bible, for that matter—do we find such words addressed to a pagan king? Certainly, we must pause to consider their implications.

Once again, if we read the passage carefully we avoid the mistake of coming to hasty conclusions. The Lord said to Cyrus,

"For the sake of my servant Jacob,

> and Israel my chosen,
> I call you by your name...."
> (Isaiah 45:4)

Cyrus was not *the* Servant of the Lord. He was *a* servant called by the Lord for the sake of "my servant Jacob."

Turn back to chapters 42 and 43. God had determined to punish his blind, disobedient servant (42:24), but that was not the end of the matter. God had also said to Jacob,

> "Fear not, for I have redeemed you;
> I have called you by name, you are mine.
> When you pass through the waters I will be with you;
> and through the rivers, they shall not overwhelm you;
> when you walk through fire you shall not be burned,
> and the flame shall not consume you."
> (Isaiah 43:1−2)

God had promised to "gather" his sons "from afar." The people "who are blind, yet have eyes, who are deaf, yet have ears" are still his people.

> "You are my witnesses," says the Lord,
> "and my servant whom I have chosen...."
> (Isaiah 43:10)

By the wonder of divine redemption, God would show his people "a new thing." Even though they did not call upon him (43:22), still he was willing to forgive.

> "I, I am He
>> who blots out your transgressions for my own sake,
>
> and I will not remember your sins."
>
> (Isaiah 43:25)

In a glorious song of the promise of redemption addressed to "Jacob my servant, Israel whom I have chosen," the Lord proclaims the ultimate deliverance of Jacob (44:1–8).

Cyrus was to be the servant who brought about the next stage in that redemptive program. God had used the Babylonians to punish Jerusalem. God would use Cyrus to overthrow the Babylonians. God had allowed a Babylonian king to destroy the temple. God would use Cyrus to bring about the rebuilding of Jerusalem and the temple.

Cyrus was not the Servant of the Lord. He was God's shepherd, God's anointed, who accomplished God's will on behalf of the servant Israel.

3

Some students of the Servant Songs are convinced that the prophet himself was the Lord's Servant. Even the Ethiopian considered the possibility: "About whom, pray, does the prophet say this, about himself or about some one else?" (Acts 8:34).

There is certainly truth in this interpretation. One of the reasons why students have had so much difficulty trying to reach a satisfactory conclusion to this whole vexing problem is simply this: it is not a question of one correct and several incorrect interpretations; rather, there are several facets of truth in the various interpretations, any one of which looked at by itself appears to be correct.

The prophet was the servant of the Lord. In the 49th chapter we read these revealing words:

> And now the Lord says,
> > who formed me from the womb to be his servant,
> to bring Jacob back to him,
> > and that Israel might be gathered to him. . . .
> > > (Isaiah 49:5)

Obviously, the person who is speaking considers that he has a divine election ("formed me from the womb") to be the Lord's servant. This idea was expressed in verse 1, and the qualifications of the servant—a mouth like "a sharp sword," a being like "a polished arrow"—are set forth in the words that follow.

We may be puzzled by the words, "And he said to me, 'You are my servant, Israel, in whom I will be glorified' " (49:3). However, we must understand the concept "Israel" in the Bible. The term can be used to refer to the people as a whole, or to a part of the people, or to an individual. Israel as a nation had been a blind and disobedient servant. The prophet had been ordained by God to be a servant in whom the Lord would be glorified.

If this discussion doesn't seem clear, let's read on and seek more light before we close our minds. The servant—whoever he might be—protests: "I have labored in vain, I have spent my strength for nothing and vanity . . ." (49:4). But the Lord who formed him from the womb says, "It is too light a thing [possibly we should read this as a question, "Is it too light a thing?"] that you should be my servant to raise up the tribes of Jacob and to restore the preserved of Israel; I will give you as a light to the nations, that my salvation may reach to the end of the earth" (49:6).

Now it seems certain that the servant is not Israel. Rather, the servant is one chosen by God to raise up the tribes of Jacob and to restore the remnant of Israel.

Yes, and even more: he has been made a light to the Gentiles. How true those words have proven! One of the books that God has used across the centuries to bring Gentiles to know him and worship him is the prophecy of Isaiah. The Ethiopian was only one of countless Gentiles to whom Isaiah has been a light.

Some would counter: "No; the prophet is not talking about an *individual*. He is talking about the *righteous remnant,* those of the nation Israel who went through the period of suffering and oppression and captivity and who remained faithful to the Lord." I don't think so. God is speaking to his servant who is to *serve* this righteous remnant. Listen:

> "In a time of favor I have answered you,
>   in a day of salvation I have helped you;
> I have kept you and given you
>   as a covenant to the people,
> to establish the land,
>   to apportion the desolate heritages;
> saying to the prisoners, 'Come forth,'
>   to those who are in darkness, 'Appear.' "
> (Isaiah 49:8–9)

These words are not addressed to the prisoners. They are addressed to the servant for the sake of the prisoners. By the servant, "the Lord has comforted his people" (49:13).

> The Lord God has given me
> > the tongue of those who are taught,
> that I may know how to sustain with a word
> > him that is weary.
>
> > > (Isaiah 50:4)

It seems that the prophet was persecuted for his obedience as the Lord's servant. According to Jewish tradition, Isaiah was finally executed by the wicked king Manasseh. The tradition may well preserve a memory of what happened to the prophet. But listen to his own words,

> The Lord God has opened my ear,
> > and I was not rebellious,
> > I turned not backward.
> I gave my back to the smiters,
> > and my cheeks to those who pulled out the beard;
> I hid not my face
> > from shame and spitting.
>
> > > (Isaiah 50:5—6)

Every obedient servant of the Lord can expect persecution. The servant Jesus told his followers, "If they have persecuted me, they will also persecute you" (John 15:20). Nonetheless, the Lord's faithful servant knows that the Lord will deliver him. Jesus said, "In the world you have tribulation; but be of good cheer, I have overcome the world" (John 16:33). The prophet said,

> Who is my adversary?
> > Let him come near to me.

> Behold, the Lord God helps me;
> who will declare me guilty?
> (Isaiah 50:8–9)

4

In the earlier chapters of this portion of Isaiah, we saw that the servant of the Lord was Israel—a blind and disobedient servant. In the middle chapters we have seen that the servant of the Lord was the prophet—a servant who did not disobey, even though he knew frustrating disappointment and bitter persecution. When we come to the closing chapters, particularly the stanzas extending from 52:13 through 53:12, we seem to see someone else, someone who is neither the nation nor the prophet. He is the Servant of the Lord in a sense that no one else ever was or could be. The entire portion is quoted at the beginning of this study. Let us read it through once again, carefully, and then let us note some of the details that are set forth in the stanzas.

The servant was not impressive at the beginning. Many were astonished at him. He was marred in appearance. He had no form or comeliness, no desirable beauty. He was despised and rejected by men. Yet the prophet initiates these comments by proclaiming that "he shall be exalted and lifted up" (52:13).

What is there about this particular servant that leads the prophet to say such things about him? Let us read on, with great care, paying particular attention to the pronouns that are used. "Surely *he* has borne *our* griefs and carried *our* sorrows; yet *we* esteemed *him* stricken, smitten by God, and afflicted." There are two distinct entities here, "he" and "we." "*He* was wounded for *our* transgressions, *he* was bruised for *our* iniquities; upon *him* was the chastisement that made *us* whole, and with *his* stripes *we* are healed. All *we* like sheep have gone astray; *we* have turned every one to his own way; and the Lord has laid on *him* the iniquity of *us* all" (53:4–6).

Obviously—if words mean anything—the servant of the Lord in this passage is not Israel. Rather, he is doing something for Israel. Obviously the servant is not the prophet. Rather, the prophet includes himself with Israel by using the word "we." If the prophet had been contrasting Israel and the servant, he would have used "you" and "he." If the prophet had been speaking of himself and Israel, he would have used "I" and "you." Note carefully that the prophet does not say, "With *his* stripes *you* are healed," nor does he say, "With *my* stripes *you* are healed." He says, clearly and simply, "With *his* [the servant's] stripes, *we* [you, the nation, the disobedient servant; and I, the servant who was called by the Lord to sustain the weary with a word; both of us] are healed."

The prophet is not speaking of himself. He is indeed speaking of someone else, someone who is the sin-bearer, someone who "poured out his soul to death," who "bore the sin of many" (53:12), someone who did this not because of the oppression of wicked men, and certainly not because he was a man of violence and deceit (53:9). Rather, "it was the will of the Lord to bruise him; he has put him to grief" (53:10). When this servant "makes himself an offering for sin," "the will of the Lord shall prosper in his hand; he shall see the fruit of the travail of his soul and be satisfied" (53:10–11).

In other words, the Servant of the Lord presented here does something for "us"—for Israel, for the prophet, and even for the Gentiles to whom the prophet was sent as a light—something which we could not do for ourselves. He carried our sins; his chastisement made us whole. With his stripes we are healed.

5

Who is this servant? Jesus Christ claimed to be the servant of the Lord. He did not, so far as the record indicates, make the specific claim that he was the servant portrayed in the 53rd chapter of Isaiah. He simply said that he came not to be served but to serve, and to give his life as a ransom for many (Mark 10:45).

The early church picked up the word "servant" and applied it to Jesus. The apostles called him "the servant of God" (Acts 3:13, 26; 4:27, 30). Just as Philip, when he was asked, "About whom did the prophet speak, about himself or some one else?" began with this passage and preached Jesus as the Servant of the Lord, so the church throughout the centuries has found Jesus Christ to be the fulfilment of the perfect Servant of the Lord, the sin-bearer through whose stripes we are healed.

Jesus said to his apostles, "No longer do I call you 'servants' ... but I have called you 'friends' " (John 15:15). But his apostles called themselves "servants." Paul, especially, used the term "bond-slave of Jesus Christ."

All of God's people are his servants. Faithless, disobedient Israel was "the servant of the Lord." The righteous remnant of Israel was his servant. The prophet who spoke these words was his servant. Jesus Christ was his servant.

Who is the servant of the Lord? He is the person whom the Lord has called to make known to the nations the truth about God's redemptive love. Some servants are faithless in that calling. Some are faithful, and by them the world has been blessed and received light. The more faithful the servant, the more perfectly he fulfils the divine purpose in that calling. However, there is one Servant who stands apart from all others. He is the Servant who so perfectly fulfils the will of the Lord that he is able to take upon himself the sins of the rest of us who call ourselves servants. Because of his willingness to suffer to the uttermost, he accomplished the redemptive purpose of God. He made himself an offering for sin. With his stripes we are healed. To him alone belongs in its fullest meaning, the title *The Servant of the Lord*.

CHAPTER TWO

ISRAEL IN HISTORY

When we hear the word "Israel," one of two identities usually comes to mind. Those of us who have a biblical background—who were brought up in an environment where the Bible had some place, even a small one, in our development—think of Israel as the people of the Old Testament. They lived in a time "way back there." At some point in the distant and foggy past they disappeared. Others, who are more inclined to think in terms of the present day, think of Israel as a small nation in the Middle East. Depending on our emotional make-up and, to a lesser extent, our knowledge of the facts, we think of Israel as a brave little state standing up to the mighty Arab coalition, a modern David-and-Goliath story; or we think of Israel as the trouble-maker who invaded the lovable and sleepy Middle East, drove the Arabs out of their homes and territory, and continues to engage in a policy of terrorism and expansion.

The Bible presents us with a considerable amount of detail about Israel. Three-quarters of the Bible is the Old Testament, and at least 95 percent of the Old Testament is about Israel. We also find Israel mentioned a fairly large number of times in the New Testament. More important than the amount of space given to Israel in the Bible, though, is the way the subject is presented. The Bible does not give us a simple history of a person—tribe—nation called by this name. Rather, the Bible presents Israel as something to which we all belong. What happened to Israel, in a sense, happened to us. Our religious faith involves us in the faith of people whom God called his "chosen." Our worship not only is drawn largely from the cultic acts of ancient Israel, particularly the Psalms, but many of its most moving and deeply spiritual experiences are expressed in terms of involvement in Israel's experiences. This is why we keep the reading of the Scriptures as part of our worship: when we read of God's work in the midst of his people in days of old, we suddenly see him at work in our midst.

We stand in the stream of God's activity through the centuries whereby he was able to make known his will, his love, his redeeming purpose. He did all this by calling into his service a people who was to receive this revelation of himself, to profit from it, and to transmit it to future generations. Insofar as every servant of God belongs to Israel, Israel never ceased to exist. Now I realize that that is a very complex statement, and we shall discuss it fully in our fourth study. At present, let me state it simply as an observation that we are going to consider and a premise that will determine somewhat the direction of our discussion. If we want to know what God has been doing all these centuries, if we want to know what he is doing today, we must understand what Israel is. For it is through Israel—and, I believe, only through Israel—that God makes known what he has been doing and what he plans to do with this world.

So we start off with a fact: There is such a people in the earth, in the history of this planet, as Israel. This people came on the scene at a certain point as a historical entity; it constituted a family, then a tribe, and then a political state—or rather, a peculiar combination of a religious and political state. This people continued for a certain period of time, chronologically speaking, but then something happened. The political state ceased to exist, but the religious group did not. It continued, and indeed it still continues, in one form as Judaism and in another form as the Christian church. Both religious communities trace their heritage to the Israel of the Old Testament. This much is fact.

If we want an explanation of the fact, we must look to the Bible. There is no logical reason why Israel should have developed the great religious, moral, and social concepts that lie at the heart of the Judeo-Christian tradition. There is no logical reason why Israel should have continued to exist. The Bible explains it as the work of God. The Bible presents Israel as the people through whom God has made known his saving purpose.

1

We begin with the events that led to the formation of Israel. The first of these, beyond debate, is the call of Abraham.

Abraham—or Abram, as he was then called—lived in Ur, an important city in ancient Babylonia. His parents worshiped "other gods" (Josh. 24:2), probably the gods of Mesopotamia. One day another god spoke to Abram. It was the God of the Bible, Yahweh, the Lord. He said:

"Go from your country and your kindred and your father's house to the land that I will show you. And I will make of you a great nation, and I will bless you, and make your name great; so be a blessing. I will bless those who bless you, and him who curses you I will curse; and in you all the families of the earth will be blessed" (Gen. 12:1–3, RSV mg).

The promise contained in these words was repeated several times. Abram was getting old, and he was childless. How could God's promise be fulfilled? Seeing no way, Abram planned to adopt his slave Eliezer as his son. But the Lord said: "This man shall not be your heir; your own son shall be your heir" (Gen. 15:4). Then God took Abram outside and said, "Look toward heaven, and number the stars, if you are able to number them. . . . So shall your descendants be" (Gen. 15:5). God went on to say,

"Know of a surety that your descendants will be sojourners in a land that is not theirs, and will be slaves there, and they will be oppressed for four hundred years; but I will bring judgment on the nation which they serve, and afterward they shall come out with great possessions. As for yourself, you shall go to your fathers in peace; you shall be buried in a good old age. And they shall come back here in the fourth generation . . ." (Gen. 15:13–15).

If we were to take the time to read through the rest of Genesis, we would find many other details that relate to this promise. The promise was repeated to Isaac, who was Abraham's natural son. It was repeated to Isaac's son Jacob. It must have been told and retold, for we find it showing up throughout the Old Testament.

Abraham's grandson Jacob was in many ways a most unlikable man, an "operator," a "wheeler-dealer." He almost met his match in his uncle Laban when he went back to the old ancestral region to get a wife, but Jacob managed to win that contest with the help of some trickery both on his part and on the part of Rachel, one of his wives. Jacob and his family were returning to the land of Canaan, where God had located Abraham; and when they came to the ford of the river Jabbok, Jacob wrestled with "a man." We are not told many of the details, but for Jacob it was an experience that changed his entire life. He was convinced that he had "seen God face to face" (Gen. 32:30). But the most important fact is to be found in a seemingly little incident. The "man" asked Jacob his name, and when he replied, the "man" said, "Your name shall no more be called Jacob, but Israel" (Gen. 32:28). So "Israel" came into existence. The name was passed on, not just to one son, but to all twleve of Jacob's sons. They came to be known as the "sons of Israel," then "Israelites," and finally their descendants were simply "Israel."

One of Jacob's sons was Joseph, a spoiled brat who was his father's darling and who loved to keep that fact prominent before his brothers. How they hated him! At last they decided to get rid of him, and as "chance" would have it, a caravan was passing by, so they sold Joseph. His beautiful coat, which his father had given him to show his favoritism, the brothers smeared with the blood of a kid. Joseph was taken to Egypt, and Jacob, when he saw the garment covered with blood, cried in his bereavement (Gen. 37:2–35).

Joseph's brothers thought they had seen the

last of him, but God had other plans. After a time of testing and persecution, Joseph came to the attention of Pharaoh. Egypt was a mighty nation, but Pharaoh was troubled with dreams. Joseph was called in to interpret them. He foretold seven years of great abundance to be followed by seven years of famine. Joseph therefore advised the king to appoint a man to be director of the Agricultural Emergency Administration—or whatever they called it in those days. Pharaoh liked the idea, and Joseph got the job. He became the savior of Egypt. More than that, he became the savior of his own brothers as well as his father. The famine, you see, extended even to the land of Canaan. When Jacob sent his sons to Egypt to buy food, Joseph recognized his brothers, but they didn't recognize him. After playing with them a while and giving them a hard time, he at last made himself known to them. As a result, Jacob too was brought to Egypt, as were all the members of the clan:

> All the persons belonging to Jacob who came into Egypt, who were his own offspring, not including Jacob's sons' wives, were sixty-six persons in all; and the sons of Joseph, who were born to him in Egypt, were two; all the persons of the house of Jacob, that came into Egypt, were seventy (Gen. 46:26–27).

Looking back over the events years later, Joseph was able to say to his brothers, "... you meant evil against me; but God meant it for good, to bring it about that many people should be kept alive, as they are today" (Gen. 50:20).

This, in brief, is the account of the events leading up to the formation of Israel. It was not yet a

ISRAEL IN HISTORY

nation. It was a family, a clan, a group of people who were the offspring of Jacob, who was called Israel. For the moment these people were guests in Egypt; later they would become slaves.

2

The second stage of our story has been called "The Birth of a Nation." The Israelites had become Hebrew slaves. The reigning Pharaoh was attempting genocide by an edict intended to kill all the male babies of the Hebrews, but Moses was spared through a scheme worked out by his mother. He was "found" by Pharaoh's daughter, who adopted him, and his mother became his nurse. So Moses grew up as an Egyptian. At heart, however, he was still an Israelite, and later, when the occasion arose, he cast in his lot with his people. As a result he was outlawed. He escaped to the wilderness of Sinai, where he married and raised a family.

Once again God issued a call, this time to Moses. God wanted him to go back to Pharaoh and say, "Let my people go." The story is familiar, so we can omit the details (Exod. 3:4–12:41). The last of the ten "plagues" which God inflicted on Egypt through the hand of Moses, though, requires our attention. God said he would pass through the land, and the first-born in every home would die. The Israelites, however, were to kill a lamb and splatter some of its blood on the doorposts and lintel of their houses. When the Lord saw the blood, he passed over that house, and the first-born was spared. This event came to be known as the "Passover" (Exod. 12:13, 27).

Actually, a bit more occurred than I have included in this simple account. The preparation for the Passover started about two weeks before the event. Everyone knew what God planned to do. The selection of the lamb was to take place on the tenth of the month; the sacrifice and the sprinkling of the blood, along with the first Passover meal, were to take place on the fourteenth of the month. All Israel was to be ready for the exodus. That event has been handed down from generation to generation, even to our own time, in the *Seder,* the Passover ritual of the Jewish people: "We were slaves in Egypt, and with a strong hand and an outstretched arm the Lord our God brought us out from there."

It wasn't quite that easy. After he had given the Hebrews permission to leave, Pharaoh had second thoughts, and he pursued them with an army. The Israelites were trapped between Pharaoh's forces and the Sea of Reeds (unfortunately mistranslated "Red Sea"). Again God came to their aid and drove back the waters by a strong east wind (Exod. 14:21). The Israelites crossed the bed of the lake, the wind died down, and Pharaoh's army was trapped.

Still, Israel was not yet a nation. All an unbiased observer would have seen was a bunch of refugees, slaves who had obtained freedom, but who knew nothing about running a nation. They had a lot to learn. And God had a way of teaching them. We can read about it in the accounts in Exodus, Leviticus, and Numbers, or we can read Moses' summary in Deuteronomy.

First, they came to Mount Sinai, where God had first called Moses to deliver his people. There God gave them the "law," summarized in the Ten

Commandments (Exod. 20:1–17) and given at length in the accompanying chapters of Exodus.

What is the law? It is the instruction of God concerning the way in which his people are to walk. The Hebrew word "Torah," which is usually translated "law," really means "instruction." Israel was receiving instructions for how they were to live as God's people, his new nation.

Then God gave them the plans for the tabernacle and the ritual. He set forth details concerning the way they should worship him and how they should look on sin that was committed after they had been redeemed, how such sin could be forgiven by God's loving kindness, his "covenant love." The penalty for sin was death, but God was willing to accept a substitute, the sacrifice of a bull or a goat or two turtledoves or pigeons (Lev. 5:5–7).

We know that the blood of bulls and goats can never take away sin. The Israelites knew that too. Micah said so (Mic. 6:6–8). So did Isaiah (Isa. 1:11–17). So did other prophets. Nonetheless, the acting out of the ritual required the Israelite to confess his sin, to identify himself with the sacrificial victim, and to realize once again that he depended on God's grace for his salvation.

Christians believe that the sacrificial system described in Leviticus foreshadowed the sacrifice of Christ. The author of the Epistle to the Hebrews has done much to foster this idea (cf. Heb. 4:14–15 for the figure of the high priest; 9:1–2, 11–12 for the Holy Place; 10:11–12 for the sacrifice, etc.). Sometimes we think that the author of Hebrews has forever abolished the Old Testament (cf. Heb. 8:7–13); but if we stop to think about it, we soon see that almost all of the Old Testament cultus has been taken up in Hebrews. The New Covenant cannot be understood apart from the Old.

So a nation came into existence. Its miraculous deliverance from bondage, its law, and its worship were told and retold from generation to generation. The stories were written down and became the Holy Scriptures. In one form or another they continue to the present day, both among Jews and among Christians.

3

When God called Abraham, he gave him a promise. Abraham was to go to a land, and his descendants would possess that land, even though Abraham himself would never own any of it except a burial plot for himself and his family. In fact, it would be many years before those descendants would obtain the land.

That promise was passed down from father to son, and God repeated it to Jacob, to Joseph, and to Moses. Now that Israel was delivered from Egyptian bondage, the hope of possessing the land of Canaan once again burned in the hearts of the Israelites. God told Moses to "send men to spy out the land of Canaan, which I am giving to the people of Israel" (Num. 13:2). Twelve men went into Canaan, and when they came back, ten of them said: "We can't do it. Those people are giants and we are grasshoppers. Their cities have walls that reach up to the sky. We can't possibly capture those cities." The minority report was given by Caleb. He said simply, "We can do it." The people, however, adopted the majority report, and God said, "Not one shall come into the land ... except Caleb ... and Joshua.... But your little ones ... I will bring in, and they shall know the land which you have despised" (cf. Num. 13:27—14:31). So for thirty-eight years they remained in the wilderness on the border of the land, until the unbelieving generation had just about died off.

Then Moses was told to move on. He led the people by a roundabout route until they stood on the heights of Moab opposite the promised land. Moses died there, and Joshua took over. Let's read the account:

> After the death of Moses the servant of the Lord, the Lord said to Joshua the son of Nun, Moses' minister, "Moses my servant is dead; now therefore arise, go over this Jordan, you and all this people, into the land which I am giving to them, to the people of Israel" (Josh. 1:1—2).

Even the extent of the land of promise was spelled out:

> "From the wilderness and this Lebanon as far as the great river, the river Euphrates, all the land of the Hittites to the Great Sea toward the going down of the sun shall be your territory" (Josh. 1:4).

And the certainty of that possession was stated:

> "No man shall be able to stand before you all the days of your life; as I was with Moses, so I will be with you; I will not fail you or forsake you. Be strong and of good courage; for you shall cause this people to inherit the land which

I swore to their fathers to give them" (Josh. 1:5–6).

The theme which is sounded over and over again in the Old Testament has been called "promise and fulfilment." God had promised Abraham and his descendants the land of Canaan. God was now about to fulfil his promise. But the land was full of Canaanites! . . . Who were the Canaanites, and what was the problem?

In 1929 an archeological discovery was made at a place in the French Protectorate which is now Syria, a place called Ras Shamra. It turned out to be the ancient city-state of Ugarit, which flourished in the 15th century B.C. Among the excavated materials was a quantity of clay tablets on which were inscribed hymns and religious literature of the Canaanites. From these tablets we learn that the Canaanites were indeed Baal worshipers. We know about Baal from numerous passages in the Old Testament. From the Ugaritic tablets we learn that Baal worship was a kind of nature worship, with elements of what is sometimes described as ritual magic. The gods and goddesses could be persuaded to give their blessings, particularly rain, grain, wine, oil, and other natural benefits, by ritual fertility-acts involving what has been called sacred or ritual prostitution. There were male and female prostitutes serving in the temples. Now that sort of religious observance can be very attractive!

But the practices of Canaanite religion violated the law which the Lord had given to Israel. So when the Israelites took possession of the land of Canaan, God told them to exterminate the Canaanites. Instead, they fell into the Canaanite way of living. God sent prophets to warn his people, and these were countered by the prophets of Baal. The story of Elijah's contest with these prophets is well known (1 Kings 18). The story of that struggle is told throughout the Old Testament. From the time they entered the land under Joshua until they were taken into exile by Nebuchadrezzar, there was a continuous conflict between the words of the Lord's prophets and the attractions of Baalism. Even the language that is used in the biblical account reflects that struggle. The people are described as "going a-whoring after false gods." They "commit harlotry." "The land has committed adultery." They "sinned on every high hill and under every green grove." These are not mere figures of speech. They are expressions that came into use because they described the religious practices of Canaan. Practically every prophet in the Old Testament has something to say against this debauched religion. God has promised the Israelites that they would possess the land—but he never intended that they should share it with the Canaanites.

Why did God give them *that* land, anyway? Why didn't he pick some other place where there were no Canaanites—Uganda, or Argentina, or Delaware? If you look at a map of the ancient world, a map omitting North and South America and Australia, you will find that what we call "Europe, Asia, and Africa" is a single land-mass. These three continents were joined by the land of Canaan. It was truly a land-bridge across which the merchants, the migrating peoples, and the armies of the world had passed since before the time when men kept historical records. In the days when shipping was limited by small boats and a very short sailing season, practically all travel was by land. Canaan was the most strategic bit of land in the whole world. It seems as if God were saying, "I want my people in that land. When the merchants move back and forth, or the armies, or the peoples looking for new homes, I want them to come into contact with the people who know my redeeming love." So, in spite of the Canaanites, God put Israel in that land.

4

We now come to the story of the failure of Israel. This people whom the Lord had delivered from Egyptian bondage, nurtured in the wilderness, and given the land—a land which they had not planted, a land containing wells which they had not dug and cities which they had not built—this people turned from the Lord to serve other gods. We could illustrate this transgression from many portions of the Old Testament, but we shall focus our attention on just two of the prophets.

The first is Hosea. Through his own personal experience he received a lesson that taught him what God had gone through and was going through with Israel. God said to Hosea, "Go, take to yourself a wife of harlotry and have children of harlotry, for the land commits great harlotry by forsaking the Lord" (Hos. 1:2).

So Hosea married Gomer. She conceived, and Hosea was told to call him Jezreel, "for yet a little while, and I will punish the house of Jehu for the blood of Jezreel" (Hos. 1:4). We need not concern ourselves with the details, except to recall that this reference is to the wickedness of Jezebel and the steps which Jehu took to exterminate the line of Ahab her husband. Gomer then bore a daughter, and God told Hosea to name her "Not pitied, for I will no more have pity on the house of Israel" (Hos. 1:6). The third child was a son, and Hosea was told to name him "Not my people, for you are not my people and I am not your God" (Hos. 1:9).

If we haven't understood the story so far, perhaps the explanation in the next chapter will help:

> "Plead with your mother, plead—
> > for she is not my wife,
> > and I am not her husband—
> > that she put away her harlotry from her face,
> > and her adultery from between her breasts;
>
> * * *
>
> "For she said, 'I will go after my lovers,
> > who give me my bread and my water,
> > my wool and my flax, my oil and my drink.'"
>
> (Hosea 2:2, 5)

Gomer was a faithless wife, or worse than that, a prostitute who gave her favors for the gifts she received. But Hosea knew that the time would come when she would change her mind and say,

> "... 'I will go and return to my first husband,
> > for it was better with me then than now.'
> And she did not know
> > that it was I who gave her
> > the grain, the wine, and the oil,
> and who lavished upon her silver
> > and gold which they used for Baal."
>
> (Hosea 2:7–8)

You see, she thought Baal was the god who gave her the favors, and the gifts she mentioned are the very things that were supposed to result from ritual prostituion.

Then God said to Hosea,

> "Go again, love a woman who is beloved of a paramour and is an adulteress; even as the Lord loves the people of Israel, though they turn to other gods and love cakes of raisins [another reference to the ritual of Baal worship]...."
> For the children of Israel shall dwell many days without king or prince, without sacrifice or pillar, without ephod or teraphim. Afterward the children of Israel shall return and seek the Lord their God, and David their king; and they shall come in fear to the Lord and to his goodness in the latter days (Hos. 3:1, 4–5).

Now it is clear. God had led Hosea through this terrible domestic tragedy to dramatize what God had been going through with Israel.

That is just one prophet's way of describing the internal situation of Israel. Other prophets had other ways of saying it, but the thrust of their message is the same: the people had gotten so caught up in the worship of false gods that there had been drastic action. The people had gone after the gods of the Canaanites because of their leaders, the kings, the priests and false prophets, the judges—all in authority had gone after false gods. They must repent, or God the Lord will act in terrible punishment.

But what about Israel's greater purpose, their mission to the Gentiles. When God first called Abraham, he told him, "Be a blessing.... In you all the nations of the world will be blessed" (Gen. 12:2–3).

What had Israel done to make the rest of the world blessed? God had put Israel in the most strategic spot on the face of the earth. What had been the result? For an answer to this question, we turn to the prophet Jonah.

One day God said to Jonah,

> "Arise, go to Nineveh, that great city, and cry against it; for their wickedness has come up before me" (Jon. 1:2).

We all know the story. Jonah said: "Nineveh! No way! Give me a ticket to Tarshish—that's the other direction; I want to get as far from Nineveh as I can." So he started west. There was a storm, and Jonah was blamed for making the gods angry. So the sailors threw him overboard. He was swallowed by a great fish. But even the fish couldn't stomach Jonah: he threw him up, and Jonah was back on the shore where he started.

God told him again to go to Nineveh. He went. And he preached. And Nineveh repented. The king, the people, even the animals put on sackcloth and ashes. I don't know whether we are supposed to take that literally or not. Certainly it is a very graphic way of telling us that Jonah's preaching was terrific. Everyone was affected by it. Jonah should have felt good about it. But was he? No. He was angry (Jon. 3:1—4:1). He complained to God:

> ". . . is not this what I said when I was yet in my own country? That is why I made haste to flee to Tarshish; for I knew that thou art a gracious God and merciful, slow to anger, and abounding in steadfast love, and repentest of evil" (Jon. 4:2).

Jonah doesn't say it in so many words, but we can hear what is going on in his mind: "I knew that if I went to Nineveh as you told me and preached your word, these people would repent, and you would spare them. And they're *Gentiles!* I am an Israelite! I don't want people like them in the kingdom of God!"

God wasn't quite through with Jonah. Jonah went out of the city and sat down, and God caused a plant to come up, rather miraculously, to cast shade over him. So Jonah sat in its shade, protected from the smiting rays of the sun, and he "was exceedingly glad because of the plant."

> But when dawn came up the next day, God appointed a worm which attacked the plant, so that it withered. When the sun rose, God appointed a sultry east wind, and the sun beat upon the head of Jonah so that he was faint. . . (Jon. 4:7–8).

So Jonah sat in the sun, perspiring and complaining to God. God asked him, "What's wrong?" Jonah told him about the plant that had died so suddenly. And God answered:

> "Do you do well to be angry for the plant? . . . You pity the plant, for which you did not labor, nor did you make it grow, which came into being in a night, and perished in a night. And should not I pity Nineveh, that great city, in which there are more than a hundred and twenty thousand persons. . . ?" (Jon. 4:9–11).

Jonah, of course, was not the only one who felt the way he did. From Isaiah's phrase "a light to the Gentiles," we know that Israel's purpose was to learn from the Lord the benefit of walking in his ways and

ISRAEL IN HISTORY

to make known this blessing to the Gentiles. Israel refused to do it! Jonah's attempt to avoid the mission to Nineveh and God's reaction was the way God symbolized this fact, just as Hosea's experience was the way God symbolized the harlotry of Israel. God is a gracious and merciful God; he wants all men to know him and to know the blessings that come from serving him.

So God—reluctantly—brought punishment on his people. The kingdom had been split in two—Israel the northern kingdom, and Judah the southern. The capital of the northern kingdom was Samaria. God brought the Assyrians, whom he called "the rod in my right hand," to punish Israel for its sins and to destroy Samaria. Israel had gone further into Baal worship than Judah. One of Israel's kings, Ahab, had married a Canaanite princess named Jezebel. Jezebel had made it her goal to exterminate the worship of Yahweh. She attempted to wipe out all the prophets of the God of Israel, and she supported 450 prophets of Baal. That was in the days of Elijah. God was patient: he waited about a hundred years while his servants the prophets pleaded with Israel to repent and return to the Lord. Then he acted. The Assyrians invaded the land, besieged and captured Samaria, and carried off many of the people into captivity.

Then for about 125 years the prophets of the Lord preached to the people of Judah, the southern kingdom. Their message, in a word, was this: "You have seen what happened to your sister kingdom. The same thing will happen to you if you don't repent and worship the Lord." But in spite of their preaching—preaching that was good enough to be treasured and handed down until finally it came to us as part of the Bible—in spite of this, the people did not repent. There were a few revivals, a glorious one in the days of Hezekiah and a lesser one in the days of Josiah. Still, the heart of the people never truly belonged to the Lord. Like Gomer, Israel was a faithless and adulterous people. So God finally turned on Judah the forces of the Babylonians, the very nation that had been used by God to punish Assyria for her wicked ways. Jerusalem was destroyed, the temple which Solomon had built was burned, the capital was razed to the ground, and the people were carried off into captivity in Babylonia.

5

Captivity. Exile. That, we should think, was the end of Israel. But it wasn't! Because, you see, God is a gracious God. He is longsuffering, slow to anger, not willing that any should die. He wants all men to know him and to live in the fulness of life that he can give. Especially, he wants his people, his Israel, to be his witness. For seventy years he watched over his people in exile. He sent his prophet Ezekiel to keep a spark of faith alive, to give them hope, and to teach them to sing songs in the night. He raised up Cyrus the Persian king to defeat the Babylonians. Cyrus was a good-hearted king who took great pride in the fact that he set the prisoners free and let the captives go back to their homes. He gave the Jews permission to return to their land "beyond the River" (the Euphrates, for this is how the Persians described the region) and to rebuild their temple.

Nonetheless, they never were a kingdom again—not really. Yes, they had a king; but he was only a figurehead under a Persian governor. Then they were under governors of the Seleucids and the Ptolemies. And then they were under the Romans. For all intents and purposes, the kingdom of Israel was gone.

What did happen? The people Israel developed a great hope, a beautiful hope. They believed that one day a king of David's line would come and restore the glory of the former days. Many of the prophets testify to this hope, but we shall look only at Ezekiel. He lived in Babylonia with the exiles. He tells us, graphically, "In the twelfth year of our exile, in the tenth month, on the fifth day of the month, a man who had escaped from Jerusalem came to me and said, 'The city has fallen'" (Ezek. 33:21). It was all over! Hope was gone. But the Lord came to Ezekiel and told him that it wasn't over: "I am against the shepherds; and I will require my sheep at their hand..." (Ezek. 34:10). The leaders who were responsible for leading Israel into sin and tragedy were to be punished. But what about the sheep? God told Ezekiel:

> "... Behold, I, I myself will search for my sheep, and will seek them out. As a shepherd seeks out his flock when some of his sheep have been scattered abroad, so will I seek out my sheep; and I will rescue them from all places where they have been scattered on a day of clouds and thick darkness. And I will bring them out from the peoples, and gather them from the countries, and will bring them into their own land; and I will feed them on the mountains of Israel, by the fountains, and in all the inhabited places of the country. I will feed

them with good pasture, and upon the mountain heights of Israel shall be their pasture.... Therefore, thus says the Lord God to them: Behold, I, I myself will judge between the fat sheep and the lean sheep.... I will save my flock, ... I will set up over them one shepherd, my servant David, and he shall feed them.... And I, the Lord, will be their God, and my servant David shall be prince among them; I, the lord, have spoken" (Ezek. 34:11—14, 20, 22—24).

So when Israel returned to their land, they developed this hope. They looked for the "Son of David." Who he was and when he would come they did not know, but they believed that he would surely come. He would gather Israel together like a shepherd, and once again they would dwell in safety, serving the Lord who had once more redeemed them.

6

One day the Son of David came. He was born to a couple who were in Bethlehem to be enrolled in the census ordered by Caesar Augustus. Angels sang "Glory to God in the highest," and shepherds came to worship the one who had been born in the city of David. Wise men came from the East, asking, "Where is he who has been born king of the Jews?" Herod called in his wise men and asked them where this king was to be born; and when they replied, "In Bethlehem," the Wise Men from the East went to Bethlehem to worship him.

When this son of David grew up, he made many startling claims. The nation asked, "Who are you?"

ISRAEL IN HISTORY

Some of them followed him; some despised him. Then one day he went to Jerusalem, but he did so in a very striking manner. He told his disciples, "Go into the village opposite, where you will find a colt tied. If anyone asks you why you are untying him, say, 'The Lord needs him' " (Luke 19:30–31). They found the colt, brought it to Jesus, and put garments on it; and he rode into the city. I think he was deliberately acting out the prophecy of Zechariah (Zech. 9:9). The people recognized the action as such, and they began to cry out the words of Zechariah, "Blessed be the king who comes in the name of the Lord! Hosanna!" (Luke 19:38).

The promises had been fulfilled—or so Jesus' followers believed. But the religious leaders got busy. They turned many people against Jesus. They manipulated Pilate into trying him. Jesus anticipated such treatment. He had looked upon Jerusalem and had said:

> "Would that even today you knew the things that made for peace! But they are hidden from your eyes. For the days shall come upon you, when your enemies will cast up a bank around you and surround you, and hem you in on every side, and dash you to the ground, you and your children within you, and they will not leave one stone upon another in you; because you did not know the time of your visitation" (Luke 19:42–44).

A little later, he turned to the people and told them a parable. It was about a man who had planted a vineyard. Israel had been known as the Lord's vineyard, and Isaiah had used that figure in a very graphic message recorded in Isaiah 5 ("The Song of

ISRAEL

the Vineyard"). The figure of the vineyard can be found in the Jewish prayer-book even today, referring to Israel. In any case, this man, Jesus said, had let out the vineyard, and then he sent servants to find out how things were going. The tenants killed the servants. This happened several times. Finally he said, "I will send my son; they will certainly honor him." But they killed the son, too. Jesus said, "Then what will the owner do? He will come and destroy these tenants, and give the vineyard to others" (cf. Luke 20:9–16). In another portion of the New Testament, we read his words, "The kingdom of God will be taken away from you and given to a nation producing the fruits of it" (Matt. 21:43).

There is not much more to add. When Paul was preaching in various cities across the Empire, he made it a point to go to the synagogues and preach to the Jews first. When they continually refused to listen, he said in the city of Antioch near Pisidia, "Since you thrust it from you, and judge yourselves unworthy of eternal life, behold, we turn to the Gentiles" (Acts 13:46). At last he came to Rome. When he gathered the Jews in Rome around him, they wanted to know what this gospel was that he was preaching.

> He expounded the matter to them from morning till evening, testifying to the kingdom of God and trying to convince them about Jesus both from the law of Moses and from the prophets. And some were convinced by what he said, while others disbelieved. So, as they disagreed among themselves, . . . Paul [said], "The Holy Spirit was right in saying to your fathers through Isaiah the prophet:
>
> 'Go to this people, and say,

> You shall indeed hear but never understand,
> and you shall indeed see but never perceive.
> For this people's heart has grown dull,
> and their ears are heavy of hearing,
> and their eyes they have closed;
> lest they should perceive with their eyes,
> and hear with their ears,
> and understand with their heart,
> and turn to me to heal them.' "
>
> (Acts 28:23–28)

I think it must have broken Paul's heart to say those words. He was a Jew. His heart's desire was that his kinsmen the Jews should be saved. He said he would be willing to be damned himself, if his brothers would be brought to Christ. The closing words express his faith: "Let it be known to you then that this salvation of God has been sent to the Gentiles; they will listen" (Acts 28:28).

Still, Paul, like the God he served, refused to give up Israel. In his great epistle to the Romans, he pours out his faith for Israel in chapters 9–11. He asks, "Has God then rejected his people? By no means!" (Rom. 11:1). And he foresees a day when, although they were like olive branches that have been pruned away, they shall be grafted in again (Rom. 11:23).

> A hardening [he says] has come upon part of Israel, until the full number of the Gentiles come in, and so all Israel will be saved. . . . For the gifts and the call of God are irrevocable (Rom. 11:25–26, 29).

CHAPTER THREE

ISRAEL IN PROPHECY

When we studied "Israel in History," we began with the call of Abraham. We shall begin at the same place to study "Israel in Prophecy," for the prophecy began at that time.

> Now the Lord said to Abraham, "Go from your country and your kindred and your father's house to the land that I will show you. And I will make of you a great nation, and I will bless you, and make your name great; so be a blessing. I will bless those who bless you, and him who curses you I will curse; and in you all the families of the earth will be blessed" (Gen. 12:1–3).

Notice the use of the future tense: "I will show you ... I will make of you ... I will bless you. ... all the families of the earth will be blessed"—these are promises.

We remember other promises made by God to Abraham:

> "This man shall not be your heir; your own son shall be your heir." ... "Look toward heaven, and number the stars, if you are able to number them." ... "So shall your descendants be" (Gen. 15:4–5).

"Know of a surety that your descendants will be sojourners in a land that is not theirs, and will be slaves there, and they will be oppressed for four hundred years; but I will bring judgment on the nation which they serve, and afterward they shall come out with great possessions.... They shall come back here in the fourth generation" (Gen. 15:13–14, 16).

"I will make you exceedingly fruitful; and I will make nations of you, and kings shall come forth from you. And I will establish my covenant between me and you and your descendants after you throughout their generations for an everlasting covenant, to be God to you and to your descendants after you. And I will give to you, and to your descendants after you, the land of your sojournings, all the land of Canaan, for an everlasting possession..." (Gen. 17:6–8).

1

If we read these words carefully, we notice three things that recur in God's promises: the election or choice by God, the descendants of Abraham, and the land of Canaan.

First, God *chose* Abraham and his descendants, his "seed," to use the literal translation of the word. The purpose for that choice is clearly defined: they were to be the means whereby God's blessing would come on all the families of the earth. For the moment we are not concerning ourselves with the families of the earth; rather we want to notice the stress that is placed on the choice of Abraham and his seed. God does not once suggest that the time will come when this agreement or covenant will be abrogated. After hundreds of years it was still in force; in fact, God calls it an "everlasting covenant" (Gen. 17:7). Such is the nature of election.

Second, the purpose of God was to be carried out by the "*seed*" of Abraham. The seed was to be a "great nation," as innumerable as the stars of heaven or the sand of the seashore. Nations and kings were to descend from Abraham.

And, finally, we take note of the *land*. Which land? The land that God showed to Abraham, the land of his sojournings, the land that was to be denied to his descendants for "four hundred years," but "in the fourth generation" they would be brought "back here." It was specifically defined as "all the land of Canaan" (Gen. 17:8).

These three elements remain constant throughout the rest of the Old Testament. They are an integral part of the prophecies concerning Israel, as we shall point out in this study.

First, we look at the word of the Lord to Jacob, who, as we have seen, left the land of Canaan and went to Egypt with his family. We can assume that there was some reluctance on Jacob's part to leave the land where he was dwelling, for he knew that God's promises were tied to that land. However, God came to him in visions of the night, and said to him,

> "Jacob ... I am God, the God of your father; do not be afraid to go down to Egypt; for I will there make of you a great nation. I will go down with you to Egypt, and I will also bring you up again; and Joseph's hand shall close your eyes" (Gen. 46:2–4).

With this promise, Jacob went to Egypt. When Jacob's days were ended, Joseph's hand did close his dead eyes, and Joseph arranged for his body to be returned to the land of Canaan to be buried in the family burial-place purchased by Abraham many years before (Gen. 50:1–14). Was this how the Lord intended his promise to be kept? Was the land of Canaan simply to become the burial-ground for the descendants of Abraham? Let's read on.

Moses was raised up by God, as we have seen, to deliver his people from the bondage of Egyptian slavery. When God first appeared to Moses, he identified himself in the following terms:

> "I am the God of your father, the God of Abraham, the God of Isaac, and the God of Jacob." . . . "I have seen the affliction of my people who are in Egypt, and have heard their cry because of their taskmasters; I know their sufferings, and I have come down to deliver them out of the hand of the Egyptians, and to bring them up out of that land to a good and broad land, a land flowing with milk and honey, to the place of the Canaanites. . ." (Exod. 3:6–8).

When Moses wanted to know what he should tell the people, God repeated the same words in slightly different form:

> "Go and gather the elders of Israel together, and say to them, 'The Lord, the God of your fathers, the God of Abraham, of Isaac, and of Jacob, has appeared to me, saying, . . . "I promise that I will bring you up out of the affliction of Egypt, to the land of the Canaanites. . ." ' " (Exod. 3:16–17).

When Moses had led the Israelites out of Egypt by the power of the strong arm of the Lord, and when they had come to Mount Sinai, God again revealed himself to Moses:

> "Thus you shall say to the house of Jacob, and tell the people of Israel: You have seen what I did to the Egyptians, and how I bore you on eagles' wings and brought you to myself. Now therefore, if you will obey my voice and keep my covenant, you shall be my own possession among all peoples; for all the earth is mine, and you shall be to me a kingdom of priests and a holy nation" (Exod. 19:3–6).

There is no doubt that the same God is speaking, the God of Abraham, and of Isaac, and of Jacob. There is no doubt that he is speaking to the same elect "seed," the descendants of Abraham through his grandson Jacob. The same purpose of the choice is expressed: they are to obey his voice and keep his covenant, and they will be his "own possession among all peoples." When God said to them, "you shall be to me a kingdom of priests," he implied the purpose of the choice, for a priest is one who mediates between man and God. Israel, therefore, was chosen by God to function in a priestly capacity between God and the other nations of the world. Yes, the first two elements are the same, but what of the land? It is vaguely defined as "the land of the Canaanites."

At a later date, when it was nearing the time for the Israelites to go into that land, the boundaries were more precisely defined:

> The Lord said to Moses, "Command the people

> of Israel, and say to them, When you enter the land of Canaan (this is the land that shall fall to you for an inheritance, the land of Canaan in its full extent), your south side shall be from the wilderness of Zin along the side of Edom ... from the end of the Salt Sea on the east ... and its termination shall be at the [Great] Sea. For the western boundary, you shall have the Great Sea and its coast. ... This shall be your northern boundary: from the Great Sea ... and its end shall be at Hazar-enan. ... Your eastern boundary ... shall go down ... and reach to the shoulder of the sea of Chinnereth [the sea of Galilee] on the east; and the boundary shall go down to the Jordan, and its end shall be at the Salt Sea..." (Num. 34:1–12).

It is possible to trace most of this description on a map. A few place-names are not positively identifiable, but in general the boundaries include the territory which is occupied today by the State of Israel, Lebanon, and the portion of Syria along the coast. (At this point, I would like to state most emphatically that I am not proposing these as the boundaries for the modern State of Israel. I have not even suggested that the State of Israel is the equivalent of the biblical term "Israel." I am simply setting forth the data of a biblical prophecy concerning Israel.)

After the death of Moses, when Joshua was about to lead the Israelites into the promised land, God said to Joshua,

> "Moses my servant is dead; now therefore arise, go over this Jordan, you and all this people, into the land which I am giving to them, to the people of Israel. Every place that the sole of

your foot will tread upon I have given to you, as I promised to Moses. From the wilderness and this Lebanon as far as the great river, the river Euphrates, all the land of the Hittites to the Great Sea toward the going down of the sun shall be your territory" (Josh. 1:2–4).

Obviously the promise continued to be in force.

The day came when the Israelites wanted a king to rule over them. They told Samuel, the judge-prophet who was in a place of leadership, "You are old and your sons do not walk in your ways; now appoint for us a king to govern us like all the nations" (1 Sam. 8:5). Samuel did not like the idea, but God told him, "Listen to these people...; for they have not rejected you, but they have rejected me from being king over them" (cf. 1 Sam. 8:7). God proceeded to tell Samuel to warn them of "the ways of the king who shall reign over them" (1 Sam. 8:9).

Samuel did so. He told the people how a king would take their sons to drive chariots and be horsemen and fight wars and work for the government; he told them how the king would take their daughters, the best of their land, the produce of their fields and flocks, and the tenth of all they possessed. They were not impressed. They said, "We want a king over us, so that we may be like all the other nations" (cf. 1 Sam. 8:19–20). So, at God's bidding, Samuel appointed for them a king. What kind of kings did they get? The Old Testament gives us a rather full account.

There was Saul, the first king: he repeatedly disobeyed the Lord's commands, or, even worse, acted without seeking the Lord's will. There was David, a "man after God's heart": he was guilty of sin with Bathsheba, the wife of Uriah, not to mention the planned murder of Uriah (2 Sam. 11:2–21). The Lord, of course, was displeased with David, but David repented and God forgave him (2 Sam. 12:7–14). What is more, God had made a promise to David, and through David to Israel. Let's read it:

> " 'When your days are fulfilled and you lie down with your fathers, I will raise up your son after you, who shall come forth from your body, and I will establish his kingdom. He shall build a house for my name, and I will establish the throne of his kingdom for ever.... Your house and your kingdom shall be made sure for ever before me; your throne shall be established for ever' " (2 Sam. 7:12–16).

David's son was Solomon: it was he who built the house for the Lord, the beautiful temple that came to be known as Solomon's Temple. Solomon's address to the people and his dedication of the temple are exquisite (see 1 Kings 8:18–53). Truly, this was the ideal king, the right man to rule over God's chosen people! But Solomon lived too long. Before he died, we read of him, "Now King Solomon loved many foreign women" (1 Kings 11:1). He not only built temples so that these wives might worship their pagan gods, but even he turned to worship the gods: "For when Solomon was old his wives turned away his heart after other gods; and his heart was not wholly true to the Lord his God, as was the heart of David his father" (1 Kings 11:4).

Of course "the Lord was angry with Solomon, because his heart had turned away from the Lord, the God of Israel" (11:9). God raised up a rival who would tear the kingdom apart; and God sent his prophet Ahijah to that rival, Jeroboam, to say, "I am about to tear the kingdom from the hand of Solomon, and will give you ten tribes" (11:31). But God went on to say,

> "Nevertheless I will not take the whole kingdom out of his hand; but I will make him ruler all the days of his life, for the sake of David my servant whom I chose.... To his son I will give one tribe, that David my servant may always have a lamp before me in Jerusalem, the city where I have chosen to put my name" (1 Kings 11:34–36).

Jeroboam turned out to be the same kind of man that Solomon had been. When his son fell sick, he told his wife to disguise herself and go to Ahijah to find out what would happen to the child. As she walked in, Ahijah said to her, "Hi there, wife of Jeroboam, what are you doing dressed up like that? I've got a difficult message for you from God himself. Go tell Jeroboam the following:

> '... "Because I exalted you from among the people, and made you leader over my people Israel, and tore the kingdom away from the house of David and gave it to you; and yet you have not been like my servant David, who kept my commandments, and followed me with all his heart, ... but you have done evil above all that were before you and have gone and made for yourself other gods ... therefore behold, I will bring evil upon the house of Jeroboam" ' " (1 Kings 14:7–10; cf. 14:1–6).

There were twenty kings in the northern kingdom of Israel, and thirty-one kings in the southern kingdom of Judah, and the story is almost monotonously similar for just about all of them. The familiar epitaph became, "He did evil in the sight of the Lord, and walked in the way of Jeroboam," or "he did more evil than all who were before him," or, occasionally, "he did what was right in the eyes of the Lord . . . nevertheless the high places were not taken away."

In spite of this depressing picture, the people never seem to have lost all hope. They looked for one who would be the ideal king, and, strangely enough, they called him "David," or "the son of David." They never called him "the son of Solomon" or "the son of Hezekiah" but always "the son of David."

2

About now, I can imagine hearing someone saying, "I thought this was supposed to be on prophecy; all we have done so far is rehearse history all over again." Well, if you'll excuse my contradicting you, let me say that this *is* prophecy. So perhaps I should face the question, "What is prophecy?"

According to a popular view, prophecy is "prediction of things to come"; prophecy is "history written in advance." This may be a very common view, but it is not a correct view—at least, not in the biblical sense of prophecy. There is a vast difference between the prophets of the Old Testament and persons like Nostradamus or Jeanne Dixon. The prophets of the Old Testament did not simply predict things to come. They proclaimed truth from God. That truth had to do with the present situation, the situation in which they and the person or persons to whom they were speaking were involved.

Now, because of God's ongoing purpose, because of his faithfulness to his promise to his covenant people, there was always in the present situation an implication for the future. The prophet, for example, might say to the king, "You have sinned; because you have done so, God is going to tear the kingdom from you and give it to another." There is a future element in the prophetic word: "I will tear the kingdom from you." However, this element arises from the present situation: "You have sinned." Or again, the prophet might say, "It shall come to pass in the latter days that the mountain of the house of the Lord shall be established as the highest of the mountains." Here we have a prophecy of the future, but it arises out of the fact that the prophet has just said, "Zion shall be plowed as a field; Jerusalem shall become a heap of ruins"; and that, in turn, was a prophecy that was called forth because the people were sinning and saying, "Is not the Lord in the midst of us? No evil shall come upon us" (cf. Mic. 3:11–4:1).

The prophets were God's spokesmen, sent to give his message to Israel. They were present throughout the period of the kings. The first prophet, as commonly accepted, was Samuel, who anointed the first king, Saul. From then until Malachi—that is, until the kingdom had ended, the people had gone into exile and returned, and a semblance of restoration had taken place—there was a succession of prophets in Israel.

We can divide the prophets into three groups, each of which had distinctive characteristics. There were the prophets of the "United Monarchy," who were commissioned to proclaim God's word to the king. Actually, this succession of prophets extended almost a century beyond the split of the kingdom. Sometimes they have been called the "non-writing" prophets, for they did not leave us written works as did Isaiah, Amos, and others who have been called the "writing" prophets. The first group includes such men as Samuel, Nathan, Ahijah, Elijah, and Elisha—and many others, some not even named.

The prophets of the second group appeared just prior to the fall of the northern kingdom Israel and continued to the fall of Jerusalem. With them came the inscripturation of the prophetic word. It seems to me that this fact provides a definite indication of a change in the nature of prophecy. During the first period, the prophets were counseling the kings, chiefly bringing messages concerning sin and idolatry and urging them to repent and turn back to the Lord. But sin was too deeply imbedded in the political life. The prophets of the second period, sometimes speaking to the kings but more often speaking to the people, proclaimed a message of judgment. Because of their sins, God was going to punish the nation, starting with its rulers, its priests, its false prophets, its merchants, and all the other persons in places of responsibility. Samaria, the capital of the North, would become a heap of ruins. Jerusalem, the capital of the South, would become a hissing and a byword. The cities would be destroyed and the people killed, taken captive, or otherwise stricken by the judgment of the Lord. Yet there was a ray of hope. God was willing to forgive if men would repent. There would be a remnant, a shoot that would spring forth from the stump of the tree that had been felled. Through this remnant or shoot, God would continue to work out his redemptive purpose.

The prophets of the third group, those of the exilic and postexilic periods, were speaking to people who had gone through the terrible experience of defeat, loss of their homes and in many cases their loved ones, destruction of their nation and the holy temple, and captivity. Ezekiel lived with the exiles in Mesopotamia, and gave them encouraging words to the effect that the Lord would restore them to their land and rebuild the fallen cities. Haggai had the difficult task of urging the people who had returned to rebuild the Lord's temple. Zechariah presented a very complex series of prophecies, which included, among other things, the hope of the restoration of the throne of David. Both Ezekiel and Zechariah spoke of future periods of adversity for Israel, and both gave assurance that God would defend his people and defeat its enemies. A common theme of the prophets of both the second and the third groups was "the day of the Lord," a time when God would bring terrible and final punishment on his enemies, and establish permanent conditions of righteousness and peace for all the nations of the world. Malachi, the last of the prophets, spoke of the rising of the sun of righteousness with healing in his wings, and promised that God would send "Elijah" before that great and terrible day of the Lord.

It must be obvious that the meaning of the word "prophecy," as it is commonly used, is drawn from the activities of the second and third groups of prophets. Even then, specific prophecies are often torn out of context. Who recalls that Isaiah 7:14, for example ("a young woman is pregnant and bearing a son, and you shall call his name Immanu-El" [literal trans.]), was spoken to Ahaz when he, in terrible fear of the coalition of kings Rezin and Pekah, was about to make a pact with Assyria? Or that Micah 5:2 ("O Bethlehem, ... from you shall come forth for me one who is to be ruler in Israel") was a strong word of hope in the face of the Assyrian invasion (cf. Mic. 5:5ff.)?

The biblical understanding of the prophets, however, always stems from their contemporary setting. Hosea, whose own domestic tragedy served to help him understand how Israel had treated the Lord and how the Lord continued to love Israel, could say fervently, "Come, let us return to the Lord; for he has torn, that he may heal us; he has stricken, and he will bind us up" (Hos. 6:1). To the people who had witnessed the mighty works of God for many generations and still had rebelled against him, Hosea could say, "Sow for yourselves righteousness, reap the fruit of covenant (or steadfast) love; break up your fallow ground, for it is the time to seek the Lord, that he may come and rain salvation upon you" (Hos. 10:12). Isaiah, who became aware of the feeble national foundations and the depth of the nation's sin in the year that King Uzziah died, knew that the Lord would do to Jerusalem and her idols as he had done to Samaria and her images (Isa. 10:11), yet he believed that one day "the remnant of Israel and the survivors of the house of Jacob" would come to "lean upon the Lord, the Holy One of Israel, in truth." "A remnant will return," he declared, "to the mighty God" (10:20–21). With that remnant in mind, he uttered this beautiful prophecy:

> There shall come forth a shoot from the stump of Jesse,

>   and a branch shall grow out of his roots.
> And the Spirit of the Lord shall rest upon
>   him, ...
> and his delight shall be in the fear of the Lord.
> He shall not judge by what his eyes see,
>   or decide by what his ears hear;
> but with righteousness he shall judge the
>   poor....
> Righteousness shall be the girdle of his waist,
>   and faithfulness the girdle of his loins.
> The wolf shall dwell with the lamb,
>   and the leopard shall lie down with the kid,
> and the calf and the lion and the fatling together,
>   and a little child shall lead them....
> They shall not hurt or destroy
>   in all my holy mountain;
> for the earth shall be full of the knowledge of
>   the Lord
>   as the waters cover the sea.
>
>   (Isaiah 11:1−9)

Prophecy, in the Old Testament sense of the word, is true not because the prophets had some mysterious power to foresee the future, but because they were so fully acquainted with the Lord and his purpose. Jeremiah knew the nature of the Lord, so he was able to accept the revelation when God said to Israel through him, "I have loved you with an everlasting love; therefore I have continued my faithfulness to you" (Jer. 31:3). Because of the promises that God had made to Israel, and because of this everlasting love, it was fully credible that God should say, "Again I will build you, and you shall be built, O virgin Israel! ... Behold, I will bring them from the north country, and gather them from the farthest parts of the earth" (Jer. 31:4, 8). God had made a covenant with Israel, which they had broken. But because he was God, and his word was forever established, their disobedience could not be the end of the matter. "Behold, the days are coming, says the Lord, when I will make a new covenant with the house of Israel and the house of Judah" (Jer. 31:31). This new covenant will be one that Israel cannot break, for it will be written on their hearts. So certain was this promise, grounded in God's faithfulness, that Jeremiah could declare,

> Thus says the Lord,
> who gives the sun for light by day
>   and the fixed order of the moon and the stars for light by night,
> who stirs up the sea so that its waves roar—
>   the Lord of hosts is his name:
> "If this fixed order departs
>   from before me, says the Lord,
> then shall the descendants of Israel cease
>   from being a nation before me for ever."
>
> (Jeremiah 31:35—36)

Ezekiel, who lived with the exiles in Mesopotamia, likewise knew that God's redemptive purpose—to save the world through the seed of Abraham—could not fail. He therefore believed God when he said that he would gather the house of Israel "from the peoples among whom they are scattered, and manifest my holiness in them in the sight of the nations" (Ezek. 28:25). The "shepherds" that had been placed over Israel—the kings, the priests, the prophets—had not taken care of the sheep. Ezekiel knew that God's love could not let him forget his sheep. God could therefore entrust these words to Ezekiel,

> "As a shepherd seeks out his flock when some of his sheep have been scattered abroad, so will I seek out my sheep; and I will rescue them.... I will feed them.... I myself will be the shepherd of my sheep.... I will seek the lost, and I will bring back the strayed, and I will bind up the crippled, and I will strengthen the weak, and the fat and the strong I will watch over; I will feed them in justice" (Ezek. 34:12–16).

If we were to ask Ezekiel, "Why will the Lord do this?", his reply would be, "It is not for your sake, O house of Israel, that I am about to act, but for the sake of my holy name, which you have profaned among the nations to which you came" (Ezek. 36:22). Yet, this statement does not mean that the Lord has not acted out of love. He promises to fulfil his redemptive purpose:

> "I will sprinkle clean water upon you, and you shall be clean from all your uncleannesses, and from all your idols I will cleanse you. A new heart I will give you, and a new spirit I will put within you; and I will take out of your flesh the heart of stone and give you a heart of flesh. And I will put my spirit within you, and cause you to walk in my statutes and be careful to observe my ordinances. You shall dwell in the land which I gave to your fathers; and you shall be my people, and I will be your God" (Ezek. 36:25–28).

Looking beyond the exile, Ezekiel saw the resurrection of Israel. Well known is his vision of a valley full of bones (Ezek. 37:1). He saw the bones coming together at the command of the Lord, and then living and standing on their feet. "These bones are the whole house of Israel," the Lord told him (Ezek. 37:11). Judah and Israel were to be reunited again; they were to be one nation in the land (Ezek. 37:22). "My servant David shall be king over them," declared the Lord. "I will make a covenant of peace with them; it shall be an everlasting covenant with them; and I will bless them and multiply them, and will set my sanctuary in the midst of them for evermore" (Ezek. 37:26).

Zechariah, who uttered his prophecies after the return from exile, looked for the coming of a king. He said,

> Rejoice greatly, O daughter of Zion!
>   Shout aloud, O daughter of Jerusalem!
> Lo, your king comes to you;
>   triumphant and victorious is he,
> humble and riding on an ass,
>   on a colt the foal of an ass.
>
> (Zechariah 9:9)

Zechariah, like Ezekiel (Ezek. 38), saw that the return from exile was not to be the end of Israel's troubles. Ezekiel saw an invasion of the land by the mysterious "Gog of the land of Magog, the chief prince of Meshech and Tubal" (Ezek. 38:2–3; 39:1). Zechariah saw a scattered people long after the regathering had taken place in the days of Zerubbabel (Zech. 10:9–10). He also saw a siege against Jerusalem (Zech. 12:2); but the outcome was victory (Zech. 12:7) by the activity of the Lord, just as it was in Ezekiel's prophecy. Although the overall thrust of his message is clear, it is open to serious question whether we should attempt to chart out the details of a prophecy such as Zechariah's. He returns to the idea of an attack on Jerusalem (Zech. 14:2); but whether it is a second invasion, a second phase of the first, or simply another vision of the same, who can say with certainty? The outcome, as Zechariah sees it, is the same:

> The Lord will go forth and fight against those nations as when he fights on a day of battle. On that day his feet shall stand on the Mount of Olives which lies before Jerusalem on the east; ... On that day living waters shall flow out from Jerusalem. ... And the Lord will become king over all the earth (Zech. 14:3–9).

Malachi, the last of the prophets of the Old Testament, foretold the day when "all the arrogant and all evildoers will be stubble," and the day that is coming "shall burn them up" (Mal. 4:1). He also added, "But as for you who fear my name [the name of the Lord] the sun of righteousness shall rise, with healing in its wings." God had Malachi tell his hearers, "Remember the law of my servant Moses," and he promised, "Behold, I will send you Elijah the prophet before the great and terrible day of the Lord comes" (Mal. 4:4–5). The work of Elijah was "to turn the hearts of fathers to their children and the hearts of children to their fathers, lest I [the Lord] come and smite the land with a curse" (Mal. 4:6).

Throughout all the prophecies of the Old Testament, we see as a continuous thread the same elements that we found in the initial promise to Abraham, namely, the "seed" or descendants of Abraham

("Israel" or "the Lord's people"), the land (Canaan), and above all the sovereign choice of this seed by the Lord and the eternal covenant by which he bound himself to them.

3

Prophecy did not end with the last book of the Old Testament. There was a silent period when the heavens seemed to have become brass and the Jewish people felt that the voice of prophecy had ceased. Then one day, it sounded again in the stirring words of a man named John, surnamed "the Baptizer." During the years between the close of the Old Testament and the opening of the New, the Jews had given a name to the "son of David," the "king" who was to come. They called him "the Anointed One" or, to use their Hebrew word, "the Messiah." John said of himself that he was not the Messiah (John 1:20), but testified that he was sent to bear witness to this "Coming One" (John 1:30ff.).

Like the prophets of old, John preached a message of repentance: "Repent, for the kingdom of heaven is at hand" (Matt. 3:2). John often used language drawn from Isaiah, and he was identified as "The voice of one crying in the wilderness: Prepare the way of the Lord" (Matt. 3:3). When his hearers protested that they were Abraham's descendants, John told them, "God is able from these stones to raise up children to Abraham" (Matt. 3:9). He identified the "Coming One" in strong terms:

> "He will baptize you with the Holy Spirit and with fire. His winnowing fork is in his hand, and he will clear his threshing floor and gather

his wheat into the granary, but the chaff he will burn with unquenchable fire" (Matt. 3:11–12).

In those days, Jesus went to the Jordan to be baptized by John. In our survey of Israel in history, we saw that Jesus was hailed at his birth as the savior of his people (Matt. 1:21; Luke 2:11), the one born "King of the Jews" (Matt. 2:2). Many times during his ministry in Galilee and Jerusalem, Jesus used language reminiscent of the prophecies of the Old Testament. Crowds of people came to believe that he might be the Messiah, and the rulers of the nation began to ask him questions designed to uncover whether he believed himself to be the Messiah. He entered into Jerusalem on the last week of his earthly life in a manner that the crowd took to be a fulfilment of Zechariah's prophecy about "your king" ... "riding on an ass" (Zech. 9:9; cf. Luke 19:38). At his trial before the high priest, when he was asked under solemn oath if he were "the Messiah, the son of God," his reply was so strongly stated that the high priest declared: "He has uttered blasphemy. Why do we still need witnesses?" (Matt. 26:65). Jesus was delivered over to Pontius Pilate, the Roman procurator, for capital punishment. When Pilate interrogated Jesus, he asked him point-blank, "Are you the King of the Jews?" (Matt. 27:11). Some students think that Jesus' answer was evasive, but Pilate apparently did not think so. On the ascription placed above Jesus' head—where the criminal's offense was normally placarded—Pilate wrote "Jesus of Nazareth, King of the Jews," and he refused to soften the statement (John 19:21–22). The entire trial, both before the high priest and before Pilate, centered about the claim implied by the title, "King of the Jews."

Even his disciples thought that Jesus had come to set up the "kingdom." At one point, they wanted to "take him by force and make him king" (John 6:15). At another time, two of his closest disciples desired the seats at his right and left sides in his "kingdom" (Matt. 20:21—whether the request was actually made by them, as in Mark's account [Mark 10:35–41], or by their mother, as in Matthew's account, is beside the point; at issue is their belief that Jesus was about to establish his kingdom). After the resurrection, Jesus was again asked about the kingdom: "Lord, will you at this time restore the kingdom to Israel?" (Acts 1:6). And even though his reply may have left their question partially unanswered, they did not understand it to be a total denial, for a short time later, on the day of Pentecost, Peter declared that "this is what was spoken by the prophet Joel," and he quoted Joel's prophecy:

> "And in the last days it shall be, God declares, that I will pour out my Spirit upon all flesh. . . . And it shall be that whoever calls on the name of the Lord shall be saved."
> (Acts 2:17–21; cf. Joel 2:28–32)

All of these issues, and many others that could be added to them, are directly related to our subject, "Israel in Prophecy." They may not all be a formal table of events that were supposed to take place, but they all, without exception, are related to what the Jews, or some of the Jews, of Jesus' day thought to be the content of prophecy concerning Israel. It is impossible to limit these beliefs to the followers of

Jesus alone, for many of the ideas can be found in the rabbinical sayings, and not a few of them appear in writings discovered at Qumran.

The Jews, in general, believed that the prophecies of the Old Testament were to be fulfilled, that a king would one day sit on the throne of David, that the descendants of Abraham would again be numerous, that Jerusalem was to be the seat of the kingdom and Palestine the land of God's promise to Abraham, and that God's covenant with Israel had never been set aside. The Jews who became followers of Jesus believed, in addition, that he was the promised Messiah, the Son of David, who came to accomplish God's redemptive purpose.

It was in this role of Messiah that Jesus pronounced judgment on his people:

> "Have you never read in the scriptures:
> 'The very stone which the builders rejected
> has become the head of the corner;
> this was the Lord's doing,
> and it is marvelous in our eyes'?
>
> Therefore I tell you, the kingdom of God will be taken away from you and given to a nation producing the fruits of it" (Matt. 21:42–43).

It was in this role that Jesus proclaimed the prophecies which we call "the Olivet Discourse" (Matt., chs. 24–25; Mark 13; Luke 21), statements which were made in reply to the questions of his disciples: "What will be the signs of your coming and of the end of the age?"

It was in this role that Jesus proclaimed the desolation of the coming days:

"But when you see Jerusalem surrounded by armies, then know that its desolation has come near. Then let those who are in Judea flee to the mountains, and let those who are inside the city depart, and let not those who are out in the country enter it; for these are days of vengeance, to fulfil all that is written. Alas for those who are with child and for those who give suck in those days! For great distress shall be upon the earth and wrath upon this people; they will fall by the edge of the sword, and be led captive among all nations; and Jerusalem will be trodden down by the Gentiles, until the times of the Gentiles are fulfilled" (Luke 21:20—24).

4

Well, just where do we now find ourselves in our study of Israel in prophecy? We started out with three themes in the prophetic message: the sovereign calling of a people by the Lord God, the descendants of Israel as this chosen people, and the land of Canaan as the place where God's chosen people were to dwell, be blessed, and be a blessing to others.

In view of what happened to Israel in the New Testament, we must ask the question, Have we misunderstood any of these subjects? Was the call of God not a permanent call? Perhaps it was conditional; perhaps the fact that Israel was so frequently disobedient and backsliding was sufficient reason for God to tear up the contract. Or did we misunderstand the meaning of "the seed of Abraham"? There are, as we shall see in our next study, a number of passages in Scripture that clearly state that "seed of Abraham" does not necessarily mean the physical descendants of

Abraham. Then, too, we might have misinterpreted the concept of the land. God is, after all, Spirit. His kingdom, we might infer, is therefore a spiritual kingdom; what does it have to do with geographical boundaries? Jesus certainly gave credence to this line of thought in his reply to the Samaritan woman (cf. John 4:21–24). Many Christians, therefore, have come to the conclusion that the old Israel is dead and gone, that all the promises of God concerning Israel are taken up in the church of Christ, and that all efforts to understand literally the Old Testament prophecies about Israel are doomed to failure.

I suppose some of these questions must have entered the mind of the apostle Paul. He was a devout Jew, a Pharisee of Pharisee parents, trained in Jerusalem under the great teacher Gamaliel (Rabban Gamliel); and until the time of his conversion, he was thoroughly convinced that Jesus was an impostor, a false Messiah.

Thinking about the situation of the Jews, Paul wrote in his letter to the Romans,

> I have great sorrow and unceasing anguish in my heart. For I could wish that I myself were accursed and cut off from Christ for the sake of my brethren, my kinsmen by race. They are Israelites, and to them belong the sonship, the glory, the covenants, the giving of the law, the worship, and the promises; to them belong the patriarchs, and of their race, according to the flesh, is the Christ. God who is over all be blessed for ever. Amen (Rom. 9:2–5).

Then he raised the question about "Abraham's seed":

> But it is not as though the word of God had failed. For not all who are descended from

Israel belong to Israel, and not all are children of Abraham because they are his descendants; but "Through Isaac shall your descendants be named." This means that it is not the children of the flesh who are the children of God, but the children of the promise are reckoned as descendants (Rom. 9:6–8).

Paul is completely certain that God's will is sovereign: "So it depends not upon man's will or exertion, but upon God's mercy" (9:16). Using Jeremiah's figure of the potter, Paul argues,

> Has the potter no right over the clay...? What if God, desiring to show his wrath and to make known his power, has endured with much patience the vessels of wrath made for destruction, in order to make known the riches of his glory for the vessels of mercy, which he has prepared beforehand for glory, even us whom he has called, not from the Jews only but also from the Gentiles? (Rom. 9:21–24).

So far it seems that Paul, too, has questions about the true meaning of "Israel." But let us read on.

Paul takes up the matter of the conversion of the Gentiles in chapter 10, which need not concern us for the present. Then he comes to the basic question:

> I ask, then, has God rejected his people? By no means!... But through their trespass salvation has come to the Gentiles, so as to make Israel jealous. Now if their trespass means riches for the world, and if their failure means riches for the Gentiles, how much more will their full inclusion mean!... For if their rejection means the reconciliation of the world, what will their

acceptance mean but life from the dead? (11:1, 11—12, 15).

Paul then uses the figure of an olive tree which has had "some of the branches" broken off, and a "wild olive shoot" grafted in "to share the richness of the olive tree." He uses this analogy as a means of cautioning the "wild olive branches"—the Gentiles who have been brought to God—against pride, and then he reminds them that

> even the others, if they do not persist in their unbelief, will be grafted in, for God has power to graft them in again. For if you have been cut from what is by nature a wild olive tree, and grafted, contrary to nature, into a cultivated olive tree, how much more will these natural branches be grafted back into their own olive tree (11:23—24).

This argument brings Paul to the final step in his reasoning about the future of the Jews:

> I want you to understand this mystery, brethren: a hardening has come upon part of Israel, until the full number of the Gentiles come in, and so all Israel will be saved. . . . As regards the gospel they are enemies of God, for your sake; but as regards election they are beloved for the sake of their forefathers. For the gifts and the call of God are irrevocable (11:25—29).

That is where Paul leaves the matter. He does not give us the details of when or how the restoration of Israel will happen. He does not answer all the questions we might ask. But he does leave us with this certain faith: God has not rejected Israel. There are countless prophecies in the Old Testament concerning

Israel and the land of promise which have not been fulfilled in the Christian church, and, in my opinion, can never be fulfilled in the church. They can be fulfilled only in Israel—the Israel that Paul is talking about in these chapters, as distinct from the Gentiles in the church. What shall we do with these portions of the word of God?

CHAPTER FOUR

THE CHURCH AS ISRAEL

The title of this chapter, "The Church as Israel," is expressed in an enigmatic way, and deliberately so. There are two common views about the relationship of Israel and the church, and I have worded the title in such a way as to avoid, if possible, any indication of preference for one above the other.

According to one view, Israel and the church are entirely different. The church, it is explained, is not mentioned in the Old Testament, and the present church age is a secret that God did not reveal to his prophets. The story of Israel, including prophecies of the future of Israel, has been temporarily interrupted by the age of the church, but when the church is removed from the scene, Israel's story will be taken up again, and the picture that the Old Testament prophets have given us will be completed.

According to the second view, the church is Israel. Israel was rejected because the nation refused to accept Jesus as the Messiah sent by God. The church has taken the place of Israel. Therefore, all of the Old Testament prophecies about Israel now apply to the church. There is no further place in God's plan for the Jew; if a Jew wants to share the divine blessings, he can become a Gentile and become a member of the church.

Now the problem is complicated, and that is, at least in part, because there is both truth and error in each view. In order to work our way through the problem, we must recognize at the outset that there is only one plan of salvation. It has been God's purpose ever since the creation of man to bring all men to himself, to bring about, on earth, the perfect harmony of all men, so that his will is done on earth even as it is done in heaven. There was only one Adam, not a Jewish Adam and a Gentile Adam. There is only one human race. The ultimate goal of God's redeeming love was to create in himself one new man, neither Jew nor Gentile (Eph. 2:13–16).

It is true that we read in the prophets about the time when the "nations" would come to Jerusalem to learn about the God of Israel. We know that the word "nations" is exactly the same as the word "Gentiles," both in Hebrew and in Greek, so we might draw the conclusion that Israel will continue to exist as distinct from the Gentiles. But what we have forgotten to include in our reasoning is a very simple fact: God, at the very outset of his electing Abraham, promised to make him a "great *goy*"—a great Gentile! (Gen. 12:2). God declared to Abraham, "You shall be the father of a multitude of *goyim*"—a multitude of Gentiles (Gen. 17:5). The implication seems clear: in the fulfilled plan of God, the distinction between Israel and the Gentiles would cease. One redeemed human family would remain.

So, if there is some truth in both the common viewpoints, we should try to discover that truth; and if there is error in both viewpoints, we should try to define and eliminate that error. Let's see what we can do.

1

There is a sense in which the church is *not* Israel. Most obvious, of course, is the simple chronological fact that the church exists this side of Calvary, and Israel in the Old Testament was on the other side, before Calvary was a historical event. We who claim to belong to Christ's church live in the faith that Christ has already died for our sins, has risen for our justification, and has promised to come again. The idea that the Servant of the Lord would bear their sins was only a promise to Israel of old. Here is the way the author of the Epistle to the Hebrews states it:

> For since the law has but a shadow of the good things to come instead of the true form of these realities, it can never, by the same sacrifices which are continually offered year after year, make perfect those who draw near. Otherwise, would they not have ceased to be offered? If the worshipers had once been cleansed, they would no longer have any consciousness of sin. But in these sacrifices there is a reminder of sin year after year. For it is impossible that the blood of bulls and goats should take away sin.
>
> Consequently, when Christ came into the world, he said,
>
> "Sacrifices and offerings thou hast not desired, but a body hast though prepared for me;
> in burnt offerings and sin offerings thou hast taken no pleasure.
> Then I said, 'Lo, I have come to do thy will, O God,'
> as it is written of me in the roll of the book."
>
> [Psalm 40:6–8]

When he said above, "Thou hast neither desired nor taken pleasure in sacrifices and offerings and burnt offerings and sin offerings" (these are offered according to the law), then he added, "Lo, I have come to do thy will." He abolishes the first in order to establish the second. And by that will we have been sanctified through the offering of the body of Jesus Christ once for all (Heb. 10:1–10).

According to this inspired author, the Old Testament sacrifices, indeed all the promises of the Old Testament, were but "a shadow of the good things to come." We might therefore say that while Israel lived in shadow, the church lives in reality. An integral part of the faith of the church is the belief that Christ died for our sins. Belief that the Messiah would die for the sins of the Israelite was never a part of the faith of Israel.

This basic fact, I might add, has led to statements something like the following: "In the Old Testament, Israel was saved by the deeds of the law; in the church, we are saved by faith in Christ." Or put in a slightly different way, in the Old Testament, salvation was by works; in the New Testament, salvation is by grace. These statements are not correctly stated, and therefore the contrast is not valid. Such an idea arises from confusion over certain statements in Scripture which have been selected without regard for the total teaching of Scripture.

No one in the Old Testament was ever saved by the works of the law. The very fact that the sacrifices were repeated year after year proves that they did not remove sin (Heb. 10:1–2). The scriptural term in Hebrew is "cover": the sacrifices "covered" sin. The result was "atonement," which—as the English dictionary tells us—simply means "at-one-ment." When the sacrifice had "covered" the sin, God and the sinner were "at one." There is never any indication, either in the Law or in the Prophets, that the sinner by offering sacrifices or by doing "good works" was earning salvation. In presenting the sacrifice, the sinner cast himself on God, believing that God was full of grace and mercy.

Of course, there were people who *thought* they were saved by the works of the law. That was the error that Paul was trying to combat. And it is from statements that Paul made when combating this error that the false doctrine of "salvation by works in the Old Testament" gained support. Those who thought they could earn their salvation by the deeds of the law were "legalists." Those who thought that Gentiles should be compelled to keep the law of Moses in order to be saved were called "Judaizers" (cf. Acts 15:1; Gal. 3:1–5). Paul strenuously opposed them at Antioch-on-the-Orontes, at the Jerusalem Conference (Acts 15:1–21), and in his letters to the Romans (Rom. 2:12–4:25) and to the Galatians (Gal. 1:6–4:31), as well as in other epistles.

Notice, particularly, how Paul argues against the false doctrine. He does *not* say: "Well, that's the Old Testament, that's the dispensation of works. All of that has been abolished, and we live under grace." Quite the opposite! He argues his case from the Old Testament, claiming that the Old Testament supports his position! "Was Abraham justified by works?" Paul asks.

> What does the scripture say? "Abraham believed God, and it was reckoned to him as

righteousness." Now to one who works, his wages are not reckoned as a gift but as his due. And to one who does not work but trusts him who justifies the ungodly, his faith is reckoned as righteousness. . . . Is this blessing pronounced only upon the circumcised, or also upon the uncircumcised? We say that faith was reckoned to Abraham as righteousness. How then was it reckoned to him? Was it before or after he had been circumcised? It was not after, but before he was circumcised. He received circumcision as a sign or seal of the righteousness which he had by faith while he was still uncircumcised. The purpose was to make him the father of all who believe without being circumcised and who thus have righteousness reckoned to them. . . (Rom. 4:3–12).

This is a long argument, and some may add that it is tedious. Nevertheless, there is no denying that Paul is arguing his case from the Old Testament. He does the same thing in his letter to the Galatians. We select just one statement that summarizes his argument:

This is what I mean: the law, which came four hundred and thirty years afterward, does not annul a covenant previously ratified by God, so as to make the promise void. For if the inheritance is by the law, it is no longer by promise; but God gave it to Abraham by a promise (Gal. 3:17–18).

But that is just Paul, someone may say. He is reading the Old Testament through the filter of his own bias. Well, let's see what some of the Old Testament prophets say about the sacrificial system.

Isaiah proclaimed:

> "What to me is the multitude of your sacrifices? says the Lord; I have had enough of burnt offerings of rams and the fat of fed beasts; I do not delight in the blood of bulls, or of lambs, or of he-goats" (Isa. 1:11).

Isaiah was speaking to sinners (1:15–18). He does not suggest that works of the law will take away their sins. Only the grace of God can cleanse them (1:18).

Let us listen to Amos' word from the Lord:

> "I hate, I despise your feasts, and I take no delight in your solemn assemblies. Even though you offer me your burnt offerings and cereal offerings, I will not accept them, and the peace offerings of your fatted beasts I will not look upon" (Amos 5:21–22).

Amos knows one way of securing God's pardon: "Hate evil, and love good, and establish justice in the gate; it may be that the Lord, the God of hosts, will be gracious to the remnant of Joseph" (5:15). Note the reference to God's grace.

Micah says much the same thing:

> "With what shall I come before the Lord,
>   and bow myself before God on high?
> Shall I come before him with burnt offerings,
>   with calves a year old?
> Will the Lord be pleased with thousands of rams,
>   with ten thousands of rivers of oil?
> Shall I give my first-born for my transgression,
>   the fruit of my body for the sin of my soul?"
> He has showed you, O man, what is good;

> and what does the Lord require of you
> but to do justice, and to love kindness,
> and to walk humbly with your God?
>
> (Micah 6:6–8)

Micah knows nothing of the doctrine that works of the flesh will take away sin. He calls the people to return to God, who pardons iniquity and passes over transgression (7:18).

There is no place in the Old Testament where we can find the teaching that man is saved by doing works to fulfil the law. He trusted in the mercy of God, who was, he believed, slow to anger and plenteous in mercy. It was precisely this understanding of the Old Testament that was expressed by Peter at the Jerusalem Conference. To those who insisted that it was necessary to keep the law in order to be saved, Peter said, citing his experience with the Gentile Cornelius,

> "Brethren, you know that in the early days God made choice among you, that by my mouth the Gentiles should hear the word of the gospel and believe. And God who knows the heart bore witness to them, giving them [the Gentiles] the Holy Spirit just as he did to us [the Jewish believers]; and he made no distinction between us and them, but cleansed their hearts by faith. Now therefore why do you make trial of God by putting a yoke upon the neck of the disciples which neither our fathers nor we [Jews] have been able to bear? But we believe that we [Jews] shall be saved through the grace of the Lord Jesus, just as they [the Gentile believers] will" (Acts 15:7–11).

The law was not abolished for Christians. The New Testament does not teach that we can steal and kill and commit adultery. As a matter of fact, every point of the law in the Old Testament is reiterated somewhere in the New Testament, sometimes in the very same words, and sometimes in a form which makes it more severe. For example, Jesus' application of the laws against killing and adultery in the Sermon on the Mount is more demanding than the Old Testament statement (Matt. 5:21–22, 27–28).

Perhaps it would help if we were to raise the question, "What is the law?" What do we mean when we refer to the "law" of Moses or the "law" in the Old Testament?

The word "Torah," which we usually translate "law," basically means "instruction." The "law" of Moses contained "statutes," "ordinances," "commandments," "precepts," and other teaching. Among the other matters comprising the law was the worship system, including the sacrifices and offerings set forth in the book of Leviticus. All of these were for the instruction of Israel—Israel in the Old Testament—from the day when they were given to Moses on Mount Sinai to the day when God would give a "new covenant" to Israel, a new covenant that, unlike the covenant that followed the deliverance from Egypt, would be written upon their hearts (see Jer. 31:31–34).

The author of the Epistle to the Hebrews, as we have seen, speaks of the old covenant period as "in shadow" and his own day as the time of reality (Heb. 10:1). He reminds his reader that "faith is the assurance of things hoped for, the conviction of things not seen" (Heb. 11:1), and he goes on to give a long list of examples of men and women who lived "by faith."

The Israelites, we have seen, were in bondage in

Egypt, from which the Lord "redeemed" them. That bondage is presented as being not only political, but spiritual bondage as well, and the deliverance of Israel is declared to be a judgment on the gods of Egypt (Exod. 12:12). Egypt became a symbol of sin, and the name "Egypt" was used in that symbolic meaning by the prophets. Israel was delivered from that sin, from that bondage to Egyptian gods, by the gracious act of the Lord (Josh. 24:14; Ezek. 23:8, 9, etc.). We should pay attention to the terms that are used. God "redeemed" Israel (Exod. 6:6; 15:13; Deut. 7:8, etc.); he "delivered" them (Exod. 6:6); the Passover was "the Lord's passover" (Exod. 12:27). Moses, because of the part he played, is associated with the Lord in this redemptive act, so that the people "believed in the Lord and in his servant Moses" (Exod. 14:31; cf. 19:9). Paul could even say of Israel that they "were baptized into Moses" (1 Cor. 10:1–3). The Passover became a type of Christ, and the sprinkled blood of the Passover lamb (Exod. 12:13) became a type of the blood of the New Covenant (1 Cor. 5:7, etc.). The Passover-Exodus, then, is the great redemptive act in the Old Testament.

The law, let us note carefully, was given *after* the deliverance of the people. It was *not* given as something to keep in order that the people might be delivered. It was given to those who had been redeemed. Why? When the Ten Commandments were given, they were introduced with the words, "I am the Lord your God, who brought you out of the land of Egypt, out of the house of bondage" (Exod. 20:2). We may assume a causal or logical sequence: "Because I brought you out of Egypt, you shall therefore have no other gods before me." The law was intended to spell out the way God's people were supposed to live because they had been redeemed.

This intent applied not only to the "moral" law but even to the "ceremonial" law, or the entire sacrificial system. Sacrifices and offerings, as prescribed by the laws contained in Leviticus 1–7, were not given to Israel as a means of obtaining redemption but as a means of "covering" (as we have noted above) the sins which were committed by the nation, its leaders, and its people. If we were to look for a New Testament counterpart, we would find it in the fact that forgiveness for believers who confess their sins is available *through the blood of Christ* (1 John 1:6–10). We should note, particularly, that the sacrifices in Leviticus were for sins of ignorance, sins of inadvertence, sins of temper or hot blood. They were never intended for cold, calculated sins, which are described as "sin of the high hand." For the man who presumed on the goodness of God, who felt that he could go ahead and sin and then obtain forgiveness, there was no sacrifice. He was to be put outside the camp, "cut off," treated like a Gentile (Num. 15:27–31).

It is with such "high-handed" sin in mind that prophets like Isaiah, Amos, and Micah point out the uselessness of offering sacrifices. Israel's sins had been committed in full knowledge of their consequences. The people had presumed on the Lord, had said, "The Lord is with us; nothing can ever happen to us," and had gone ahead with their abominable acts. With such an attitude they were no longer acting as God's people; in fact, he said, "You are not my people" (Hos. 1:10). God's people are supposed to live in accordance with the instructions they receive from God. They are supposed to "keep the law," not in order to *become* his people, but because they *are* his people. And when they transgress his law, as human beings are prone to do, they know that they can come in repentance, confessing their sins and offering a sacrifice, and God will receive them back to himself, because they are his people and he is their God.

The people of the Old Testament—certainly the godly, the righteous persons—lived "by faith." They looked back to Abraham their "father," whose faith was reckoned as righteousness (Gen. 15:6). And they looked ahead to the fulfilment of the promises which God had made through the prophets. The author of Hebrews says of them, "These all died in faith, not having received what was promised, but having seen it and greeted it from afar, and having acknowledged that they were strangers and exiles on the earth. . ." (Heb. 11:13).

After rehearsing the faith of a long list of Israelites, the author of Hebrews makes a startling statement: "All these, though well attested by their faith, did not receive what was promised, since God had foreseen something better for us, that apart from us they should not be made perfect" (Heb. 11:39). Thus he both compares and contrasts the faith of Israel and the faith of the church.

The faith of Israel in the Old Testament is remarkably similar to the faith of the church in the New Testament. For this reason, the New Testament writers could draw repeatedly from the Old Testament to set forth their teachings. Like the church, Israel is the people called out of the "nations" by God, not because of superior value or size or goodness, but because of God's love (Deut. 7:7-8). Like the church, Israel was "redeemed" by God's work of redemption, the sign of which was the blood of the Passover lamb sprinkled on the doorpost. Like the church Israel received the law—except that in the church it is given by the Spirit of God in the heart, whereas in Israel it was carved on tablets of stone. Like the church, Israel was given a burning hope, the hope of a glorious day when sin and all its brood would be removed and when righteousness would prevail. Like the church, Israel connected this glorious future with the "son of David."

But in spite of the similarities, Israel in the Old Testament, as we have seen, is *not* the church.

2

Now, there is a sense in which the church *is* Israel. If we fail to note the differences between Israel and the church, we move into great confusion. On the other hand, if we fail to note the identity of the church as Israel, we also stray into error. Only by clearly understanding the relationship of each entity to God's purpose can we hope to approach the truth.

God called Israel "my people" (Exod. 3:7, etc.). Because of their gross sin, God pronounced that they were not his people, but he also foretold a day when they would be reclaimed and once again be called "my people" (Hos. 1:10; 2:23). Paul applies the words of Hosea to the Gentiles in the church,

> ... even us whom he has called, not from the Jews only but also from the Gentiles? As indeed he says in Hosea,

> "Those who were not my people
> I will call 'my people,' . . ."
> (Romans 9:24—25)

Paul, therefore, understood that Hosea was referring to Gentiles when he spoke of "those who were not my people," and that Hosea was referring to Gentiles who would become, like Israel, God's people.

In Exodus (19:6), Israel is described as "a kingdom of priests." These words are applied to the church by John: "He has made us to be a kingdom, priests unto God" (Rev. 1:6).

"Christ" is a word that has come to us from the Greek word *christos,* "anointed." It was a translation of the Hebrew word *mashiach,* which also means "anointed." The Hebrew word gave us our English word "messiah." I mention these facts because our English Bible, as commonly translated, uses the word "Christ" in numerous passages where "Messiah" would make the meaning a bit clearer to us. At the same time, I wish to point out that the title that was given to Jesus, and which then became a part of his name, "Jesus Christ," is a term drawn from the concepts of Israel. The first Christians were Jews who believed that Jesus was the long-awaited Messiah.

Paul takes this term "Christ" or "Messiah" and uses it over and over again in his letters to gentile churches, letters such as Ephesians, Colossians, and Philippians. The inference is clear: Jesus is the Messiah for the Gentiles in the church as well as for Israel.

We have seen that Paul wrote Galatians to refute the heresy of Judaizers who were teaching that it was necessary for Gentiles to be circumcised and to keep the law of Moses if they were to be admitted to the church. At the conclusion of this epistle, Paul says,

> For neither circumcision counts for anything, nor uncircumcision, but a new creation. Peace and mercy be upon all who walk by this rule, upon the Israel of God (Gal. 6:15—16).

Certainly, the term "Israel" is not used here of the Old Testament people. There are about 68 places in the New Testament where the word "Israel" is used. Of these, about 65 refer to Israel of the Old Testament. The other three, including the verse in Galatians, refer to the church.

In his letter to the Ephesians, a gentile church, Paul makes a very important statement:

> Therefore remember that at one time you Gentiles in the flesh, called the "uncircumcision" by what is called the "circumcision," ...— remember that you were at that time separated from Christ, alienated from the commonwealth of Israel, and strangers to the covenants of promise, having no hope and without God in the world. But now in Christ Jesus you who once were far off have been brought near in the blood of Christ. For he is our peace, who has made us [Jews and Gentiles] both one, and has broken down the dividing wall of hostility, by abolishing in his flesh the law of commandments and ordinances, that he might create in himself one new man in place of the two, so making peace, and might reconcile us both to God in one body through the cross, thereby bringing the hostility to an end.... So then you are no longer strangers and sojourners, but you are fellow citizens with the saints and

members of the household of God... (Eph. 2:11–19).

It begins to be clear that the term "Israel" is not to be confined to the blood descendants of Abraham. It would seem that in New Testament times there was, at least among some Jews, a pride in their ancestry. Such pride would be understandable, for in the reforms instituted by Ezra, Jews were instructed to put away their gentile wives (Ezra 10:2–4), a demand based on a passage in the law (Deut. 7:1–5). Now, we can see the advantage of avoiding mixed marriages, both in the days when Israel was entering into the land of Canaan and in the time when a remnant of Israel was returning from exile. But if we study the history of Israel carefully, we quickly come to the conclusion that purity of the blood-line was not the primary intention of God in calling Israel to be his people.

When Israel went out of Egypt, they went out "a mixed multitude" (Exod. 12:38). Provision was made in the Ten Commandments for "the sojourner who is within your gates" (Exod. 20:10). When Israel entered into Canaan, many other peoples joined them: the Gibeonites, some of the Canaanites and Hittites, and most likely many other tribal strains. Ezekiel refers to Israel saying, "Your father was an Amorite, your mother a Hittite" (Ezek. 16:3). Moses married an Ethiopian (Num. 12:1). Ruth, the ancestress of David, was a Moabitess (Ruth 1:4). It would be hard to prove that Israel was of pure descent from Abraham. Yet, that seems to have been the claim of some. John the Baptist faced such a belief when he called on the people to repent and added, "Do not presume to say to yourselves, 'We have Abraham as our father'; for I tell you, God is able from these stones to raise up children to Abraham" (Matt. 3:9). Jesus came up against the same idea. He had said, "I know that you are descendants of Abraham," and the Jews answered proudly, "Abraham is our father." Jesus then replied, "If you were Abraham's children, you would do what Abraham did..." (John 8:39). Direct descent from Abraham is not the essential; rather, living according to the faith of Abraham is what is expected of Israel.

Paul, too, grappled with this problem in his long passage on Israel in the epistle to the Romans. He first describes the Jews, his kinsmen:

> They are Israelites, and to them belong the sonship, the glory, the covenants, the giving of the law, the worship, and the promises; to them belong the patriarchs, and of their race, according to the flesh, is the Christ.... But it is not as though the word of God had failed. For not all who are descended from Israel belong to Israel, and not all are children of Abraham because they are his descendants.... This means that it is not the children of the flesh who are the children of God, but the children of the promise are reckoned as descendants (Rom. 9:4–8).

Paul clearly distinguishes between the physical descendants of Abraham and those who are "reckoned" as his descendants.

This passage may sound, if we ignore the rest of what Paul has written in Romans 9–11, as though he has completely identified the church, particularly the gentile portion of the church, with Israel. We have already seen, however, that he maintains a clear-cut distinction in Romans 11.

The church, then, is in a sense properly called "Israel." "Israel," we have learned, was the concept of a people called by God to be his servants in his great redemptive work. Israel was to receive revelations of his will from him and to be guided by these revelations. In the course of history, and in the light of these revelations, Israel developed a hope that was centered in the activity of God and at the same time worked out by a human agent. Specifically, the human agent was the "Son of David," the "king" who was to come in the name of the Lord. It was repeatedly made clear, though, that the ultimate achievement of the purpose of God was not through human effort but by God, who used his servant to accomplish his purpose.

All of the elements of this concept of Israel can be applied to the church. God revealed himself to the church—in fact, the revelation to the church was better, more complete, more readily discernible, than was the revelation to Israel, for "the word became flesh" and lived with the first members of the church. The "Servant" offered his life as a ransom for his people. God caused the church, by its failure to achieve the ultimate goal of its mission immediately, to develop a hope. This hope was expressed in many of the terms drawn from the prophetic utterances of the Old Testament, but another item was added that makes it distinctive: the church associated the realization of its hope with the return of Jesus Christ. To the church, he was the "Son of Man" coming in the clouds (cf. Dan. 7:13; Mark 13:26), as well as the messianic king coming to establish his kingdom. The church believed that the "new covenant" which Jeremiah had foretold (Jer. 31:31) had been given by

Jesus Christ; and the very term became part of the eucharistic ritual, taken over from the words of Jesus spoken at the Last Supper (1 Cor. 11:25). The church also believed that the outpouring of the Spirit prophesied by Joel (Joel 2:28–32) had been fulfilled on the Day of Pentecost (Acts 2:1–4, 16–18).

A great many more illustrations could be drawn from the New Testament, supported by passages from the Old Testament, but we have seen enough to draw this conclusion: the church can properly be identified with the concept of "Israel"—if not in all details, then surely in the main points.

3

Well, I have spent part of this chapter showing that the church is *not* Israel, and part of the chapter trying to demonstrate that the church *is* Israel. Just what am I trying to say?

Let's go back to Genesis 12, to the call of Abraham. That is where it all began. Someone may ask, "What about Adam and Eve?" At that point, we are dealing with the entire race. The same is true if we attempt to begin with Noah. But with Abraham, for the first time, God called out an individual to participate in his great, unfolding plan to bring the human race back to himself.

First, there is a divine choice, a selection or election, based solely on God's will. Abraham was at that time not a worshiper of the Lord. In fact, the Bible seems to tell us that he didn't even know the Lord's name (Exod. 6:3). His parents and grandparents worshiped pagan gods (Josh. 24:2). There was no reason why God had to choose Abraham: he had no particular moral excellence, no humanistic qualifications; it was simply a matter of God's sovereign choice. But Abraham responded to the call in faith, and he obeyed the divine command. These elements, then, become a paradigm. We find them both in the Old Testament and in the New, identifying the people of God's choosing. To his people God continues to reveal himself and his will, either through the prophets and apostles, or through Jesus, the incarnate Word, or through the scriptural accounts of his redeeming acts in past time. And his people respond in faith and obedience. If they lack faith—by that I do not mean simply that they have weak faith but rather that they have no commitment to the Lord at all—they are not counted as his people. If they have faith, even though it is weak and even if they disobey, he is willing to hold on to them; he asks only that they repent and come to him for forgiveness. These are God's people. They are called Israel, the servant of the Lord, and they are called the church, the elect of God.

Second, God promised a blessing in that initial call. God promised to bless Abraham, to make him the father of a great multitude, to make his name great. This promise was repeated in many ways, and God's intent to fulfil it was demonstrated many times. Abraham's seed did indeed become a great multitude. Kings were produced in that progeny. Israel became a kingdom. In the New Testament, the blessing continues. By including gentile believers in the term "seed of Abraham," the church made the number still greater. The blessings of God were poured out on his people.

Third, there was the purpose in the choosing:

Abraham was to "be a blessing." Through his descendants, all the world was to be blessed. If we are looking for missionary activity in the Old Testament, we have great difficulty finding it. Israel was not engaged in a campaign to convert the Gentiles. In fact, outside of Jonah there is no Israelite missionary, and Jonah became one against his will. On the other hand, the gentile world quickly became the object of the church's evangelistic zeal. The incentive was twofold: first and foremost was the command of Jesus Christ to "disciple the Gentiles" (cf. Matt. 28:19–20; Luke 24:47; Acts 1:8); and second was the great hunger which the Gentiles manifested, once the proclamation of the gospel was turned in their direction.

But this brief contrast does not give the complete story. The fact is that Israel was indeed a blessing to the gentile world. The basic principles of the law of Moses have influenced moral and legal standards in many lands. The worship of Israel has greatly affected gentile worship, particularly in the church, but to no little extent in Islam as well. The concept of Holy Scripture has brought forth other sacred scriptures. Not all holy books, of course, are due to Israelite influence; but some are, most notably the Koran and the Book of Mormon. Hebrew psalms have influenced gentile poetry and gentile song. Hebrew proverbs are widely quoted in many parts of the world. Old Testament personalities and stories have made tremendous contributions to gentile literature. Most of all, Jesus of Nazareth, a Jew according to the flesh, gave the religion which bears his name to the world, Jew and Gentile alike. Truly, Abraham's descendants have been the source whereby the nations of the world have been blessed.

Jesus berated the Jewish nation for their failure to produce fruit for which they were brought into being. As Christians, we must, of course, accept that verdict. Certainly, if we understand Jesus' rebuke as applying to Jewish efforts to propagandize the gentile world with their faith, it is a valid criticism. However, when we talk about "the purpose of God," we must accept the axiom that he is omniscient. He certainly knew how his calling of Israel would turn out. The idea that God must wait until he sees how man will respond before he can make his next step is not compatible with the biblical view of God. God knows the end from the beginning. We must, therefore, examine the "failure" of Israel in this light.

Let us remember that for over a thousand years Israel had been taught to be "different," "a peculiar people" (Deut. 14:2 KJV). Such isolationism was essential for Israel's preservation, and it was due to the failure to observe the principle of separation from the nations (particularly the Canaanites) that Israel turned to worship false gods. In the light of this separationism, Jonah's attitude toward the repentance of Nineveh must have seemed quite reasonable to him. After the exile, when through intermarriage and daily concourse with Gentiles the Jews could quickly have lost their separate existence, Ezra emphasized more strongly than ever the need to be a separate people. Others followed his principles. Efforts of Hellenizing Jews to remove signs of their Jewish identity were met by rigorous efforts on the part of the "Pious" or "Separatists" to enforce every detail of the law—and this meant particularly, having no religious or social contact with Gentiles.

In the fulness of time, with the advent of God's

servant Jesus Christ, the church was called to take up the purpose which had been Israel's. The first church, entirely Jewish, had great difficulty breaking through the barrier of separationism. Paul and Barnabas were severely criticized for their work among Gentiles. Peter, and even Barnabas, turned back from this venture and had to be rebuked by Paul (Gal. 2:11–14). Eventually, though, the church was able to break down the "wall of partition" (Eph. 2:14) and proclaim God's redeeming love to all the world. When this purpose has been fulfilled, at least to the extent that God has designed it, then Israel will once again be restored to the original purpose for which God chose Abraham and his seed—so Paul teaches us in Romans 11:25–32.

At that time, if we have understood the Scriptures correctly, Israel, having been restored to the land that was promised to Abraham, will become the fountainhead of the knowledge of the Lord. The law will go forth from Zion. Nations will come to Jerusalem to be instructed in the way of the Lord. Kings of the earth will render tribute to the messianic King on Zion's holy hill. And the evangelization of the whole world, which has been done by the church on a large but at best partial scale, will at last be commensurate with the love of God. Is this not what Paul means when he says of Israel,

> So I ask, have they stumbled so as to fall? By no means! But through their trespass salvation has come to the Gentiles, so as to make Israel jealous. Now if their trespass means riches for the world, and if their failure means riches for the Gentiles, how much more will their full inclusion mean! (Rom. 11:11–12).

4

Well, what will be the outcome? How does the story end? We started in the book of Genesis, and we shall conclude in the book of Revelation.

John, the seer of Patmos, was taken up to heaven, that he might see how it all would end (Rev. 4:1). He writes,

> I looked, and behold, a great multitude which no man could number, from every nation, from all tribes and peoples and tongues, standing before the throne and before the Lamb, clothed in white robes, with palm branches in their hands, and crying out with a loud voice, "Salvation belongs to our God who sits upon the throne, and to the Lamb!" (Rev. 7:9–10).

The multitude that the Lord promised to Abraham as his "seed" is now indeed as numerous as the stars in the heaven or the sand on the seashore. And they are from "every nation."

Toward the end of the book, John gives us a picture of the final outcome of God's redemptive activity:

> Then I saw a new heaven and a new earth; for the first heaven and the first earth had passed away, and the sea was no more. And I saw the holy city, new Jerusalem, coming down out of heaven from God, prepared as a bride adorned for her husband; and I heard a great voice from the throne saying, "Behold, the dwelling of God is with men. He will dwell with them, and they shall be his people, and God himself will be with them; he will wipe away every tear from their eyes, and death shall be no more, neither shall there be mourning nor crying nor

pain any more, for the former things have passed away" (Rev. 21:1–4).

Then John tries to describe the holy city. But how can you describe what no one has ever seen before? You use images, likenesses that call up something of the glory of your vision; but they remain a scanty, incomplete presentation of the truth. Here is John's description:

> In the Spirit he carried me away to a great, high mountain, and showed me the holy city Jerusalem coming down out of heaven from God, having the glory of God, its radiance like a most rare jewel, like a jasper, clear as crystal (Rev. 21:10–11).

So John continues, talking of a jasper wall, of a city of pure gold as clear as glass, of gates of pearl, of streets of gold. The city was twelve thousand stadia (about 1500 miles) in each direction—"its length and breadth and height are equal" (Rev. 21:16)—but was it a giant cube, an apartment-house to end all the gigantic structures ever devised by man? or a giant pyramid, like that on the back of an American dollar bill? or a ball-shaped satellite? John doesn't say, for even the word "foursquare" (*tetragōnos*) is capable of describing only a two-dimensional figure. Perhaps it's better that way. When we begin to think about it, we realize that any attempt that we make to explain the imagery reduces its possible meaning. John's language goes far beyond our ability to paint it or fashion it in earthly materials.

One thing John said, though, is of particular importance for our study:

> It had a great, high wall, with twelve gates, and

at the gates twelve angels [or messengers], and on the gates the names of the twelve tribes of the sons of Israel were inscribed.... And the wall of the city had twelve foundations, and on them the twelve names of the twelve apostles of the Lamb (Rev. 21:12–14).

John doesn't explain the need for these "great, high walls." They kept no one inside, and they kept no one out, for "its gates shall never be shut by day—and there shall be no night there" (Rev. 21:25). Those who could not enter the holy city were not kept out by closed gates; rather, it was their own unclean, false character that made entry into the holy city impossible (21:27).

There was only one wall; not two, not a Jewish wall and a gentile wall, but just one wall. On the gates were the names of the twelve tribes of Israel, and on the foundations were the names of the twelve apostles of the Lamb. Without any one of them the wall would not be complete. The Israel of the Old Covenant and the church of the New Covenant are joined there, to make one holy city, with one Lord, one faith, and one baptism, one God and Father over all (Eph. 4:4–6).

There are significant differences between Israel and the church. But when we look at them from the viewpoint of eternity, the differences are only temporary. In God's plan, and by God's righteous servant, men and women and children from every nation, Jew and Gentile alike, will live in peace and security and light in the holy city.